an indian journey

an indian journey

By

Waldemar Bonsels

Illustrated by

Harry Brown

Ross & Perry Inc.
Washington, D.C.

© Ross & Perry, Inc. 2001 All rights reserved.

Protected under the Berne Convention. Published 2001

Printed in The United States of America
Ross & Perry, Inc. Publishers
717 Second St., N.E., Suite 200
Washington, D.C. 20002
Telephone (202) 675-8300
Facsimile (801) 459-7535
info@RossPerry.com

SAN 253-8555

Library of Congress Control Number: 2001094925
http://www.RossPerry.com

ISBN 1-931641-96-X

☻ The paper used in this publication meets the requirements for permanence established by the American National Standard for Information Sciences "Permanence of Paper for Printed Library Materials" (ANSI Z39.48-1984).

All rights reserved. No copyrighted part of this publication may be reproduced, stored in a retrieval system, or transmitted, in any form or by any means, electronic, photocopying, recording, or otherwise, without the prior written permission of the publisher.

CONTENTS

	PAGE
I. PANYA, ELIJAH AND THE SNAKE	1
II. CANNANORE, THE FISHERMEN AND THE SEA	22
III. A NIGHT WITH HUC, THE MONKEY	41
IV. VALARPATTANAM LAGOON	60
V. JUNGLE FOLK	77
VI. FEVER	103
VII. IN THE HILLS	124
VIII. THE THRONE OF THE SUN	140
IX. THE REIGN OF THE BEAST	157
X. A TYRANT OF THE MARSH	173
XI. MANGALORE	196
XII. WOMEN, MISSIONARIES AND BRAHMINS	216
XIII. THE LAST FIRE AND THE OLD SPIRIT	239
XIV. HOME!	259

AN INDIAN JOURNEY
FULL PAGE ILLUSTRATIONS

FACING PAGE

PLATE I · · · · · · ·	FRONTISPIECE
PLATE II · · · · · · · · · ·	36
PLATE III · · · · · · · · · ·	53
PLATE IV · · · · · · · · · ·	100
PLATE V · · · · · · · · · ·	117
PLATE VI · · · · · · · · ·	164
PLATE VII · · · · · · · · ·	181
PLATE VIII · · · · · · · · ·	212

I··PANYA, ELIJAH AND THE SNAKE··I

WHEN I arrived at Cannanore in the blessed province of Malabar, the Hindu Rameni led me in front of his house which he wished me to rent from him during my stay there. To get my first glimpse of it he and I had to join forces and work our way together through the wild tangle of the garden. It was in the usual style of the European houses in India, a one-storied bungalow with a high-pitched roof, overhanging eaves and a wide veranda across the whole of the front. Said Rameni:

"This is my dearest possession on earth. I have kept and tended it carefully, and for seven years no human being has set foot in it. The last tenant was Sahib John Ditrey, an English officer of great renown, to whom every soldier drawing near had to do obeisance. He spent his days happily under this roof, and would still be living here had not the government sent him and his retinue to another station."

I contemplated the great rooms. They were empty for the most part, and overgrown with a rank vegetation, and they harboured a whole world of animals, whose number and variety aroused my highest expectations.

"Harmless beasts," said Rameni genially. "Most of them will probably leave; they don't like the society of human beings. But, Sahib, you won't eat your heart out with loneliness. You have brought plenty of company along, a dog, a boy, and a cook. And I will let you have chickens if you want."

Rameni's command of English was so remarkable that I positively felt my hair stand on end under my sun-helmet.

"You are an Englishman, too," he continued, after a lengthy panegyric upon Sir John Ditrey.

I told him that I was a German, and he offered ready consolation.

"I never heard of Germany before," he observed; "but its people are said to be generous, and probably it is wealthier than the British Empire."

Taking the hint, I enquired what rent he was asking for his house. Thereupon he began to talk so eagerly of other matters that my fears grew. At length, however, I was able to bring him to the point. He began a calculation, adding up with suppressed emotion all the losses he had sustained during the seven years in which the house had stood untenanted. Listening in silence, I watched the

AN INDIAN JOURNEY

doings of a tribe of white ants which had skilfully tunneled the joists and boards of the flooring and the timber work of the walls.

"I shall not be in your way," I thought to myself. "Your kingdom shall flourish and reach to heights undreamed of under my rule, and I will be to you a wise prince and a faithful comrade."

The morning sunlight streamed in through the thicket of palms outside the window as through green veils with jagged patterns. Again I felt that illusive sense of happiness steal over me which had set my heart a-tremble the moment I set foot on the soil of India and breathed in its perfume and warmth and light.

"Do not fear, Sahib," said Rameni, . . . he continued making mute account on his outspread fingers, almost beside himself with doubts, hopes and expectations.

I told him I was brave, and for the tenth time he raised his hand to add up once more from right to left upon the thin, brown fingers. Then, forgetting everything else, he spoke breathlessly of the rise in prices and the badness of the rice crop.

"The first coolie you ask will bear me out in this," he said. "Shall I call one?"

"How much do you want?" I asked curtly. "I have heard of a house by the sea, the one in which the Collector used to live. The government will let me have it at a very moderate rent."

At this, Rameni pulled himself together with a great effort, and said the rent was one hundred rupees per annum. For the loss of the seven years he would charge me only a fourth, provided that I would pay him the full rent for three years in advance.

When I nodded assent, he turned pale.

"Sahib," he stammered, "are you making fun of your servant? It is quite true that I asked a great deal. Let us forget the seven disastrous years. I shall put up with the affliction decreed, especially since it is over now. If you will really pay me three years' rent in advance, I shall serve you faithfully for the rest of my days."

I never regretted my ready acquiescence. Though I stayed only a few months in Cannanore, I was more than repaid for my slight sacrifice, for Rameni made it a point of honour to work off the shame I had unwittingly put upon him. Almost every day he sent me a present of eggs, fruit, fish, or poultry; and he agreed to all the repairs and alterations in the house and in the garden that I asked for. Not until after several weeks, when he noticed that I was keeping a live cobra in a glass case, did he shun my company. After that he would not cross my threshold or touch my hand. It was not so much that he was afraid. I learned from a trustworthy source that he was sorry he could no longer visit me. But it did not square with his convictions that anyone should keep a god imprisoned in order to watch the deity's doings through a glass plate. Up to the time of this discovery, my acquaintanceship with Rameni remains one of the pleasantest memories of my sojourn in India.

A bullock cart brought my luggage up from the harbour, and we three—my boy Panya, my cook and myself —set to work to put the rooms with the best exposures in

AN INDIAN JOURNEY

order for the night. Panya was full of the most urgent warnings, but he had come to realise that many of his fears were identical with my hopes. The cook, a hillman from southern Mahratta who had made the acquaintance of Europeans in Bombay, had long since given up resisting the evil in me. In fact, he did not concern himself about me. He did his work with a reserved, stoical calm; cheated me whenever he had a chance; and with languid lowered eyelids awaited my destruction, which he unfailingly prophesied when I detected him doing something wrong. Nevertheless, I always felt a liking for the obstinate fellow, who was proud after his own fashion; who could not bring himself to cringe before Europeans; and who, because of his love for his homeland, cherished a hatred of foreigners. The dignity of his silent resistance contrasted nobly with Panya's pliant submissiveness; but Panya's attitude, too, proceeded not from a meanness of spirit, but from a childlike admiration for the glitter of everything that was foreign. I named the cook Pasha, for I could never remember his real name. Indeed, no one could have remembered it.

When I went on to the veranda to make sure that there was not a window in the house that was not broken, Panya was squatting on a box of books, smoking, with my hammock lying across his knees.

"It's all in holes," he said, not rising and not starting to work busily as he had used to do when he saw me coming. "Sahib, that's what comes of using a hammock for a fishing net."

"It was a splendid idea," I said in excuse.

"You didn't catch anything," retorted Panya.

I examined the floor. It had been undermined everywhere by the white ants. The flagstones and the boards shook as one walked, and sometimes one's feet sank in, destroying a whole Sodom and Gomorrah of the ant population.

"If you want to see how those creatures live, you must not disturb them," observed Panya sarcastically. "By the way," he added, "there are rats in the house, and there are cases of plague just outside Cannanore."

"We must get cats," I decided. "Go to the city tomorrow and buy some."

Panya looked at me pityingly. "Pay for a cat? There are cats running loose all over. I'm sure there must be cats in this house."

He was referring to a small variety of cat, of which I had seen plenty in Malabar; they are to be found in most old buildings. I decided, therefore, to wait. One had to be careful, since rats are supposed to be the carriers of plague, and this dread epidemic still hung on, although the rainy season had been over for some time. As a rule, plague disappears with the last rainfall at the beginning of the Indian spring, for the plague bacillus only flourishes in the damp. It appears again with the first rain after the hot season.

My account of this conversation may have given a false impression of my relationship to Panya, and of the general attitude of Europeans towards the servant class in Hindustan. I allowed Panya and everyone else who served me a great deal of personal freedom; but my sacrifice of authority, even of independence, brought a return which I have always valued more highly than any other offerings of human contact. A man's truthfulness interests me least of all his qualities. Servility is synonymous with simulation. The Englishman's treatment of the natives keeps out of sight their traits of character and suppresses their true nature. I admit that the attitude of the ruling caste of whites is essential to the maintenance of their position as rulers. But I did not go to India to be one of its rulers.

Sometimes there were exciting scenes between Panya and myself, when we wrestled with one another for the position of authority. They ended usually in the overthrow of the slave. And yet my blow and his collapse were phenomena that stood in no relation to one another. Often he broke down before I even touched him; and at the worst he was mostly able, by an artful twist of his body or some other device, to escape with no more serious consequences to himself than the derangement of his turban or his oiled head-dress. Nevertheless, he invariably went to pieces, squirmed from one corner of the room into another, and howled and wailed over my ingratitude and the reward he got for his devotion. But before evening he would take care that the burden of my guilt should not rob me of my night's rest.

"Sahib," he would say, standing erect as a pole in front of me, his features illumined with a pride and a dignity which did in truth fill my heart with gratitude, "Sahib, how could you forget yourself like that?" His face expressed such sorrow that I could not for the world bring myself to doubt its honesty. I would modestly explain to him the magnitude of his offence and its serious consequences; but in such cases his command of English was too poor to follow me.

"You are not getting on very well with your Hindustani," he would say with some concern; and we were both glad to have found a topic upon which we could resume the footing of our ordinary intercourse. Then would come times of a happy transformation and beautiful fellowship. While they lasted, Panya's self-renunciation went so far as to place the whiskey bottle on the table without having filled it with water, so that I could tell exactly how much he had stolen.

I had now been ten months in India, and during that time had had a fine dog for a companion, besides Panya and Pasha. Elijah was now a year old, so that I had the opportunity of educating him myself and watching over his development. Pity it is so hard to tell from a puppy two months old what its breed is and what manner of a dog it will turn out to be. But I like people who see the best side of things and assume that others are as good as themselves until the contrary has been proved. From their example I have come to see Elijah as the Perfect Dog. I will not dwell on his external appearance, especially since time may still bring forth some changes. There is no doubt, however, that he has an excellent appetite and sleeps well. He is extremely cautious, and always shuns danger. He does not attack strangers, and suppresses his watchdog alertness to the utmost, which I much appreciate as I am often engaged in mental work that requires concentration, and barking would be disturbing. His devotion is so great that he gives it to everyone he meets. Without self-interested motives I must pay tribute to his extraordinary strength of will, the foundation of true character. Neither threats nor promises can induce Elijah to heed my wishes, or anyone else's. He never dirties up in the garden or in the street, and he relieves us of all trouble to serve him his meals.

I am sorry I have not yet been able to establish decent relations between him and Panya. Evidently Panya is indulging his traditional oriental notions of the nature of a dog. There is no doubt that he lacks all deeper appreciation of breed.

"Sahib, what sort of a pig are you bringing home?" he exclaimed when I arrived with the newly acquired Elijah.

"He is dusty and the collar has drawn tight round his neck," I answered. "He'll be all right when he's been washed."

"Are you going to wash him?" asked Panya, staring alternately at me and at Elijah with wide-open eyes.

"He's an extremely clever dog, and will be most useful to us," I said, a trifle chilled by Panya's reception of us.

I gazed reflectively at Elijah who had stormed the doorsill, and in his helpless ardour presented a fascinating picture of innocent energy.

If all the seed I planted in the youthful soul of Elijah has not borne fruit, Panya is surely to blame, for the boy has never tried to conquer his contemptuous opinion of the dog. All educational influence upon an unawakened mind

AN INDIAN JOURNEY

must depend for its success upon the joint labours of every one of the housemates. While Elijah continues to lack a basis of support in Panya, and while Panya continues to regard Elijah as the source of all evil, I shall not derive from either of them all the joy I had promised myself.

The evening caught us unawares at the close of this first day in Cannanore. Panya rummaged in the boxes for candles, and turned everything upside down. The mosquito curtain for my bed was at the bottom of the largest box, for when we were packing up, Panya had of course begun with this, so that it was buried beneath all the rest.

Long after Panya fell asleep, I remained on the veranda, waiting for the moon and coolness to come. From the motionless drapery of the trees, shrubs and flowers in the garden came a sultry breath, an intoxicating mixture of perfumes. Every plant was in bloom, and a voluptuous exuberance of life forced itself upon me, into my very blood. The whole atmosphere, resounding with the chirp of the crickets, was charged with this quiet, mighty urge to rank bourgeoning, and was so still that the light of my candle never flickered, only quivered as if from the compression of the saturated air. From the palm groves somewhere in the distance behind the garden, sounded wind instruments in a Hindu temple, mingled with a monotonous leaden jangling. The singing that went with the music betrayed the growing inebriation of the priestly chorus.

I closed my eyes, and was staggered by a picture that

the music evoked from my earliest childhood. I recalled how I had been lured out of our garden into the road by a strange sound, the like of which I had never heard before. It came from a distance, from where the lime trees along the road seemed to grow closer together at the village, and veiled everything in mysterious shadow. Forgetting that my mother told me to stay in the garden, I ran out into the sunshine, leaving the garden gate open behind me. In front of a farm I saw two tall, gloomy-looking men under a tree, surrounded by a group of flaxen-haired village children. The men had black beards and wore long cloaks. It was they who were making the music, which came screaming from the grey bags into which they were blowing, and which overwhelmed me with the first and greatest experience of my childhood. I remember distinctly that in the turmoil of my blood I had to hold on to something to keep from falling. I realise now that at that hour a poignant restlessness began to stir in my soul, and that I was then being vouchsafed the first glimpse of my destiny. Even to-day my yearnings pursue this animal-like wail full of impetuous desire, as if in hope of salvation. When I hear its call, I leave the near and the familiar for the strange and the uncertain, the house for the highway, and the home for the world.

When I opened my eyes, a large brown moth was sitting on the handle of the copper candlestick, looking dazed and helpless at the incomprehensible light. After a time the insect began to move its wings slowly; its eyes full of fear and motionless darkness were suffused with the light of the sacred flame. Its powerful wings were borne lightly through the air, the air which I breathed with so much difficulty, and which bore down so oppressively upon my breast. I now noticed for the first time that the veranda had become peopled, that a winged race of nocturnal vagabonds had made themselves my guests. They all came mysteriously out of the green wall which surrounded me and the house. Behind this wall the moon must have risen, for in the warm mass of vegetation I could now distinguish lighter and darker patches, could discern the patterns of the fan-shaped palms, and the mighty outlines of the banana leaves, thrusting skywards like the clubs of slumbering giants or drooping brokenly like a torn vesture. The sky was invisible. I blew out the candle, and silently a dim, magical twilight rose and spread around me, as if the world were cut off from the light by a green sea of glass.

Of all human endowments, man's thoughts are the noblest. Those who were born in the night, who in their journey through the world are ever in search of a light which shall not perish, become most alive at night, as though in the darkness a mysterious dread awakens them to redoubled energy. From them nothing is hidden; the road to the future is as open to them as the road to the past; they penetrate into the secrets of submerged generations, into the calyx of the flowers, and into the chambers where their lovers sleep. The small things with which they concern themselves in everyday life do not quench their ardour to seek out the essence of God. Their triumph is in the infinite, their unconscious goal is eternity. The stronger they are, the more earnestly they strive for order, the sister of knowledge; and it is their earthly task to discover the links between the spirits of those who now live and those who have passed away.

As I let my thoughts run on like this, I heard strange noises from inside the house, a shuffling and a tapping, a scraping along the walls, small crackling sounds among the rafters. At intervals I heard the cries of animals, weird war cries, or else love plaints. Whether these cries came from the house or from outside was hard to tell. I relighted the candle in order to escape the uncertainties of the dark. When I went to bed, the moon had fully risen. I was tempted to stroll in the moonlit garden, but the dangers were too great in this strange place that had been left deserted so long.

Panya was lying asleep in the hall on his cocoanut mat. His snoring reassured me; it was the only familiar sound in the seclusion. In the background a low shadowy form vanished noiselessly through an open door of the room adjoining the garden. I thought of following it but did not. When I entered my bedroom I found Elijah curled up on the bed.

The woodwork of the windows had rotted, and in places was broken; the window panes had disappeared. Here, too, the impenetrable wall of vegetation closed the view to the outside and kept the air from coming in. The flowers in the room spread a strong, almost tangible scent, sweet and noxious, while out in the moonlight the crickets shrilled louder and louder.

I examined my revolver, though I knew there was nothing wrong with it, and moved my bed away from the

AN INDIAN JOURNEY

window. It was hard for me to have to awaken Elijah; I knew that the least disturbance was a grave insult to him, and on this night of uncertainty I did not want my only companion to be in a bad humour. But he merely muttered crossly without really awaking, and went on sleeping on the floor. I put out the light, as it would draw too many insects, retired within the protection of the mosquito netting, and tried to sleep.

Outside, the noises grew louder and more passionate every minute. The animation of the strange animal world communicated itself to my blood and excited me, so that I felt I should soon have to give up all hope of sleep that night. My thoughts busied themselves with the numerous changes and repairs necessary for a long stay in the house. They put me out of sorts, as trifling practical matters are apt to do when they forcibly replace the contemplation of higher and more harmonious relations. By degrees, however, my thoughts lost their grip; outlines became hazy; and through closed lids I had the vague impression that the room had grown lighter, and the chirp of the crickets had dissolved into a sultry and oppressive sea of air in which I was drifting lifelessly. I sank into a heavy sleep as if drugged with opium.

A gentle pressure at my side awoke me with a start, and I lay rigidly in the position in which I had awakened until I recognised Elijah, who had crept under the cover of my bed carrying the mosquito net before him. Had not the fearful din in the room been even greater than my anger, I should certainly have taught my innocent dog an entirely new kind of somersault. But in a moment I real-

AN INDIAN JOURNEY

ised instinctively that it was in sheer terror that Elijah had come to me. He was trembling violently and was whimpering in deadly fear. So I let him be, pressed him to me, and tried to discover the cause of the extraordinary noise which filled my room.

It was now almost light in the room; the moon had risen so high in the heavens that the light came into the house over the tops of the palm trees. At first I could not make out anything. The patch of light on the floor and the pale rays athwart the air blinded me. Then I saw that the floor was alive with a swarm of large excited rats, gathered as if for an attack on one side of the room. In the corner, facing them, cowered a family of cats, small long-haired beasts, with their young. Between the two some dead rats were lying, while several wounded ones were crawling painfully along, squeaking lamentably, and leaving a trail of blood as they moved. It was plain that the cats—there were four or five fully grown and a number of kittens—were hard pressed and greatly alarmed. They were fighting a battle of desperation against the superior forces of the rats. There was something wildly terrifying in the menace of their spitting and miauling even to the overmatching strength of their enemies, and their postures reminded me of an infuriated panther. It was evidently an old feud, which had gone on for a long time in the house, and to-night had broken out into a bloody battle, one of very many, perhaps, that had preceded it. The position may once have been reversed. In former days, perhaps, the cat tribe had ruled absolutely, oppressively tyrannising over the rats, until the rats gained the upper hand, which they seemed to hold now.

The rats moved slowly forwards, with hideous cries of sanguinary rage. The weird illumination and the well-nigh empty room, with corners shrouded in semi-darkness, strangely distorted my sense of size and distance; it seemed to me that huge black monsters overtopping me in size were advancing to do battle, and that I was looking on from a distant hill-crest.

One of the cats (an old, experienced tom-cat, it seemed) sprang forwards to the defence with a long, low bound—a wild leap that alarmed and thrilled me. The cat did not rely much on its teeth, but dealt blow after blow with its claws, deftly, stubbornly and with fatal precision. At first the rats scattered at the leap, save one only, which, struck down by the cat's paw, writhed screaming on the floor and was now left unnoticed. The gleaming eyes of the cat, as it crouched with head close to the ground, were watching the host returning to the onslaught. They advanced slowly, with a hideous squealing that voiced both their fear of death and savage rage of battle. But when the cat sprang among them again, it did not effect another panic. The rat singled out for attack fixed its teeth in his lip. In a transport of pain, he struck out fiercely but devoid of aim, leaped high into the air and twisted about on the floor, while the rat, almost torn to shreds and streaming with blood, clung tenaciously to the cat's mouth and was jerked to and fro, up and down. Almost breathless with horror, I watched the shadowy forms of the companions of the rat that had immolated itself for the tribe imbed their teeth from all sides into the flesh of the fighting feline. Presently I saw close to the wall another troop of rats advancing to attack the cats huddled in the corner. They came forwards in a compact mass like a slowly moving shadow; the terrible wailing of the dying tom-cat in the centre of the room seemed to keep time with their ghostly march like martial music, awesome and challenging.

As if upon a preconcerted signal, the shadowy coil hurled itself like lightning upon the cats; and there ensued now a second and equally fierce struggle in the darkness, a struggle which seemed to me all the more terrifying because I could not make out the details in the darkness.

A dainty little kitten, hardly realising the danger, sprang into the moonlight, gracefully leaping. Two shadows, perceptible only by their furtive movements, followed swiftly—a few moments, and the little thing was torn to shreds. At its heartrending cry of distress, its mother made a desperate effort to come to the rescue. I looked on horrified, as the dreadful assailants fixed their teeth in her body. With screams of pain, such as I had never heard from a cat, she writhed upon the floor, dragging her assassins after her as she moved, unable to render any assistance to her kitten.

Had not the battle been interrupted immediately after this in a decisive manner, I should certainly have intervened to bring it to a close. In the retrospect, I have frequently asked myself, why I did not do so at once. There is a strange fascination in watching animals fight. It is a voluptuous but not altogether wicked pleasure. It has its roots partly in a respect for the spontaneous movements

AN INDIAN JOURNEY

of Nature, and in a subconscious realisation of the truth that man can neither add to nor take away from the laws which she imposes. I remember my delight in childhood over watching a cock-fight—the exalted sense of admiration with which I awaited the event, altogether without distress or shame. My boy-mind found it hard to understand why people strove to separate fighting dogs. When a dear little pug of mine to which I was sincerely attached, had its throat bitten through by a wolf-hound, I have a distinct recollection that I regarded the ferocious victor with an emotion akin to adoration and envy of his laurels.

Now, at the very moment when, tormented with horror and pity, I had made up my mind to put a stop to the bloody battle—when I was reaching for my revolver and anticipating with secret satisfaction the instant effect the crash of a pistol-shot would have in clearing the battlefield, there issued from the dark corner behind me a sound more potent and imperious than a bark from out of the muzzle of a revolver. It was a faint hissing or rather a spitting sound, resembling the ludicrous noise geese are making when they go to meet an opponent with lowered head. But the effect of this tuneless, repulsively penetrating voice was anything but ludicrous—it was distinctly terrifying. I felt the blood congeal in my veins, and the deadly stillness that followed heightened my terror to the point of lifeless petrefaction. Then I heard, in the stillness of the room, my blood rush to my ears and a hammering of my heart so painful that I had a choking sensation. I saw the animals on the floor—dark, motionless patches. Even the death-cry of the wounded was silenced for a time

—only one huge rat, whose body had been completely ripped open, circled in the moonlight on the floor in a pool of its own blood, wrapped in its entrails. Its hoarse squeaking, combined with that hideous round dance, produced an almost comical effect of detachment and unsuspecting preoccupation.

I once heard a fakir declaim these lines in Mahratti:

> The serpent spoke beneath the heated rocks,
> Its tuneless song freezes the heart to snow,
> For from its voice protrude the eyes of death,
> As from expanses of eternal ice.

As I took them down at his dictation, I learned from him that they were of ancient origin, part of a song much in vogue with the hillmen of the Western Ghats. Now I did not think of the verses at that moment—it was as though the verses thought of me. They took possession of me in my terrible plight and again I experienced the miracle of that sublime serenity which, in moments of anguish, sometimes descends upon us like a superior and independent power outside of us.

I saw a huge snake gliding forwards. Its narrow head was perhaps a hand's breadth above the floor, and as it entered the moonlight I saw its delicate tongue flashing in and out. To my fancy, the creature seemed to be smiling.

There began now, under my very eyes, the cruel interlude of the serpent, known to and extolled or accursed by all the nations of the earth. To no other creature has been given that mysterious power of the snake which seems to

AN INDIAN JOURNEY

emanate from a soundless, inscrutable Inferno of Evil. Neither strength nor courage, neither good arms nor sturdy resolution are able, as a rule, to imperil the dominion of the serpent, for in addition to its potent magic it has that power of inspiring loathing which disarms even the hero. Apart from this power of inspiring disgust and other protective qualities that are of the essence of the snake, its movements radiate a bad charm which fascinates us like a rooted memory of the perpetual triumph of evil. Its furtive creeping is like an evil rite, its beauty suggests subtlety, its power baseness. All the qualities that make for frankness in the strong, are in the serpent alloyed with craft, for the secret satisfaction, as it were, of selfish wickedness. The elements of water, earth and air seem to forfeit their distinctive peculiarities under the influence of serpentine twinings—for the movements of the serpent are incomparable to that of any living creature. In it, the simple rippling of water is associated with the conjurations of the Magi.

The snake, desisting from its mesmeric dance that casts a spell upon all animated beings, suddenly seized in its coils a wounded rat that was still living and began to swallow its prey. Its indifference and the calm assurance of its action aroused my utmost astonishment. It hardly seemed aware that there could be any hostile power capable of harming it. Everything remained quiet in the room, except that a fine dust rustled down at intervals from the ceiling, and that the zig-zag patterns of moonlight on the floor showed a slow lateral movement.

"The earth continues its rounds," I thought, "bearing

AN INDIAN JOURNEY

me with it, bearing this predatory snake, bearing all the little dying and dead beasts within the room, and all the persons and things separated from me by an immense expanse of ocean."

Outside, Panya snored. Elijah had gone to sleep, nestling into my back. Chary of noise, I reached for the box and took out of it one of those slender Indian cigars which are as brown as peat and as damp as the sod, lighted it and awaited the dawn. My thoughts rose with the smoke-wreaths into the verdant break-o'-day and their subject was the life of men and beasts on this curious orb.

II · CANNANORE, THE FISHERMEN AND THE SEA · II

ERE dawn of day I went out-of-doors, intent upon watching the silent struggle between the red of sunrise and the greenish silver-light of the moon. I had often seen the tall, lonely palm trees on the seashore bathed in a red glow upon one side of their stems while the other still bore the argent livery of the moon. In the morning breeze, they seemed to awaken slowly, out of this cold illumination. Thus did they stand, in a glory of light and colour, at the edge of the restless sea, whose voices were greeting the advent of day.

This morning, however, I was not destined to enjoy the glorious sight, for Panya had business with me.

"Sahib," he exclaimed, when I asked him to fetch me some water, "what sort of a house is this you have taken?"

I began to describe it, but he stopped me in dismay. "I haven't slept a wink all night," he said, and the challenging distress in his eyes bordered on insolence.

"Look here, Panya," I said, as civilly as I could, "I

AN INDIAN JOURNEY

want some water for my bath. You must bear in mind the customs of my country."

He led me thereupon through the garden, without another word, despairing of convincing me that my demand was unreasonable save by ocular demonstration.

We were surrounded by all the freshness of an Indian morning in the springtime. The blossoms were brimming over with dew. Their colours were resplendent in the first light of day, so that my eyes could hardly encompass the delight of all their beauty. The reek of the wet sod and the odours of a thousand opening flowers made me dizzy with joy.

Panya, too, felt this intoxication, as if the heavenward yearning of the blossoms were uplifting his soul as it did mine. He tossed his head so that his brown nose might sniff the air, grinned in crude rapture and looked round at me. He was drinking in the freshness and the light with all his senses, his dusky, naked body shining with dew.

When we drew near the water-tank at the end of the garden, close to the palm grove, I could discern nothing at first but a towering interlacement of creepers. Not until Panya had parted these could I make out the steps leading down to the water, as if into a subterranean cave. In the dim light I noticed that the crumbling flagstones were overgrown and almost covered with rare mosses. A chill odour of decay assailed my nostrils and Panya, who seemed to have forgotten his ill-humour, whispered a word of warning as he peered into the hollow, almost in awe. His brown face beneath the white turban was framed by a

AN INDIAN JOURNEY

mass of partially opened red blossoms, each as large as a child's head. A butterfly in blue velvet rose sleepily from one of the flower-bells pendant and flew noiselessly away into the wilderness of vegetation.

"Do not descend," said Panya. "Death lurks everywhere in the shadows. I have seen the water. It is green, covered with plants. It carries flowers that have never seen a ray of sunlight. That makes them as poisonous as the snakes and the fevers here indwelling."

He suddenly recalled his grievance. His childlike eyes lost their reverent earnestness. Wrinkling his brows, he said: "What a house to take! How long are you going to stay? Let me pack up everything, that we may be ready for a return to Bijapur."

On the way back we met Pasha, the cook, who crossed the road, on his way to the house. On his shoulder he carried a pitcher of red earthenware filled with water, as he strode in the light of the newly risen sun. From the house came the reek of a wood fire. Saluting me with his free hand, Pasha marched silently past. He looked proud of his country and his duty; making me perceive that he regarded me as an interloper in the former, and that he did the latter out of regard for himself, not me. From his great velvet eyes beneath their long lashes peered the hillman's yearning for the hills. His virile carriage was a delight to see. It made me feel that the nickname I had given him was absurd. I desired to know his real name, were it only that I might repeat it to myself, this strange-sounding name hailing from a strange tribe of

AN INDIAN JOURNEY

hillmen. I had a fresh access of the peculiar sadness which never entirely left me in India, the sadness mantling the human heart whenever confronted by the Inscrutable.

Panya's delicate sensibility to all my changes of mood when touching his own interests made him aware that Pasha's silent activity pleased me. He said:

"These dogs of hillmen have a cute scent for everything edible. But I am sure he will forget to boil the drinking water, and then you will have fever to-morrow, Sahib. I must go and look after it myself."

He disappeared into the house and immediately I heard a yelp from Elijah. Although the red glow of dawn was not yet over, the sun rays were already hot. The garden was steaming, and from amid the morning mist rising through the palm grove came the song of birds mingled with the first hum of awakening insect life. I left the teeming garden and, in search of fresher air, strolled down the sandy road, reddish in tint, stretching towards Cannanore through banyan trees of immemorial age. The house was about halfway between town and sea, nearly a mile from each. I determined to pay a brief visit to the town while Panya was making my tea.

The broad highway was almost empty. A bluish haze of wood smoke rising from among the palms lay over Cannanore. The town was quite hidden by these trees, as are most of the towns and villages of the fertile Malabar coast. The quiet was so intense that I could hear the rippling of the waves on the rocky shore, and the sunlight was incredibly gentle and pleasing. A bullock cart lumbered past, rattling as it went. It was drawn by white oxen, whose huge horns, fully a yard long, swayed rhythmically above the glistening backs. The tall wheels ground their way noiselessly through the sand. A Hindu was squatting on the shaft, between the very tails of the splendid, patient beasts, his chin on his lean knees. He blinked at me shyly, without venturing a salute.

Flanking both sides of the dilapidated town-gate stood a lonely palm—one slightly inclining to the right, the other to the left. Over the flat roofs, the fanlike crowns of these trees stood out in plain umbrage against the bright sky of morning, their stems tinted red in the sunlight. Through the gate I got a glimpse of the bazaar, where a bustle had already begun. Figures, some nude and some clad in white, were moving briskly to and fro between the rows of low-roofed houses. The traders were opening their booths and displaying their wares for sale. The watchman at the gate stood up to make a profound obeisance, covering his face with his hands. I went into the bazaar, aware of the stillness and the sensation in my trail wherever I passed. Only the Brahmins stalked mutely past, without greeting and without turning their heads. Among them I detected straight-limbed men with imposing countenances. Upon their features I could read once again a distant kinship with the Teutonic races of our own Continent, discerning traits not effaced by the passage of millenniums. For ages the Brahmins ruled over this wide realm, until Moslem invaders planted the banner of the Prophet amid the palaces of their Kings, undermining step by step the dread and enigmatical Brahmin power, which none the less continues its sway in the recesses of the country, amid dark deeds of violence and hidden mysteries. In due time, however, the star of the Prophet likewise paled, together with the glory of the Moslem rulers, when the roar of the British lion reverberated across the ocean and filled the land with its uproar. On my way home, after a short town ramble, I saw the outlines of the British fort against a background of sea. Day and night the big guns point straight at the palace of the Hindu King, ready to lay it in ruins at the first sign of revolt. Beneath the silent muzzles trained upon the town linger the inconspicuous remnants of the ancient regal rule of Cannanore.

There was much to be put to rights in the house, to be sure, before it would be fit for a long stay, and over my tea I had a talk with Rameni and Panya concerning ways and means. Rameni had slipped off his shoes at the door. During our conversation he tried in vain to strike a comfortable posture in the reclining chair which he had accepted out of politeness, at my bidding. When he rose to his feet again, he arranged the folds of his white garments revealing his thin brown legs from the knees downwards.

"Everything shall be done according to your will, Sahib," he said as amiably as his atrocious English permitted. Panya looked at him with such contempt that he broke into a perspiration.

It was delightful on the veranda. An Indian spring morning (we were in the end of October) is fresh and invigorating. The sun does not grow really hot until it has

AN INDIAN JOURNEY

been up for three or four hours. Panya was in good humour after Rameni's departure.

"How the swine stinks," he said genially. "He will cheat you in everything, Sahib. If your wealth were not past counting, he would ruin you. Now I must destroy the ants—they are eating up everything. The best way to exterminate them is to pour whiskey into the cracks between the flags and ignite it. Give me a bottle, so that I can go to work when you go down to the sea."

I suggested that he try kerosene which was easily procurable in town.

Panya shook his head. "The poor creatures," said he.

After a time, a troop of old women arrived on the scene, with brooms, pails and rags. The sight of them put the guileless Elijah to flight, and I, too, fled. Only Panya stood his ground against the onslaught of these amazons, to assert his authority.

In a few days the house had been so thoroughly set in order that I might have begun a contemplative existence full of valuable impressions. Panya, likewise, readily accommodated himself to our new mode of life. Never shall I forget the glorious, tranquil spring days which ensued. To my senses, invigorated by deep sleep, came the distant call of the sea, summoning me day after day to its glittering realm. I made friends with the fishermen at Cannanore, and presently dropped into a habit of joining them at their work. Their mistrust at the outset I was able to overcome, and we had much to learn from one another.

In the gloaming and far into the night, we would sit

AN INDIAN JOURNEY

upon the black rocks of the seashore, projecting far into the waters in high, steep boulders. Often we had to leap from one rocky platform to the next, or keep our balance as we walked narrow planks, on our way to the outermost reef from which the lines were cast. Close to us, on either side, rose and fell threateningly the huge mass of waters. First, the surface was of a deep, pure blue; slowly it turned red, dazzling our eyes, until at length the sea had become deep black, so that it almost appeared as if there were a motionless, dark mirror into which the rock was being rhythmically plunged. Far behind us thundered the surf; and farther back still, the copper-coloured moon rose over the palms.

These men were mainly engaged in catching very large fish. The hooks were as thick as a child's finger and baited with the guts of the previous catch. Four or five yards above the bait, a piece of light bark was fastened to the line as a float. The fishermen whirled the hooks round their heads before throwing them out to sea, so that as much as twenty yards of line would be paid out before the bait struck the water. Then the men squatted on their haunches motionless, as if part of the rock, until a gentle tug on the line warned them of a bite. Often the swell would rise until the water almost lapped our naked feet, and the next moment it would be far beneath us. Even during the night the fishermen knew when a big wave was coming and would call in low tones a warning that I must hold fast. Then, for a few moments, the rock would disappear from view, with nothing visible but the dark and foaming waters. At first, under the circumstances, I had

AN INDIAN JOURNEY

to overcome a feeling of insecurity and even of terror. But the imperturbable calm of my associates soon steeled my courage.

The lines were never tightly gripped but always held so that they could run easily through the fingers, for sometimes a shark would bite, and the first tug might have pulled the fisherman into the water. Once when I was with them, a shark was hooked, and a loud cry instantly put them all on the alert. I saw the line paying out swiftly, like a ship's hawser when the anchor is let go; then the rope was hastily belayed to a projecting piece of rock. As a rule, in such cases, the line is lost. But sometimes, as on the occasion mentioned, it was possible to drag the shark shorewards between the cliffs. I was alarmed at the fierce energy of the captive, making an awesome struggle in its helpless state. The line was now made fast to a stake driven into the sand, without any attempt to remove the hook, and the shark was allowed to take its own time about dying on dry land. Next day the women would come to cut everything marketable from the smooth body. The flesh was not used as food.

Northward the dark rocks ended abruptly. Along the open bay the white sands stretched as far as eye could see. Here and there were clumps of palms growing down to the water's edge, especially where streamlets debouched. In the nearer distance, within reach of the town, the native boats lay beached on the sand. Beyond the farthest of these, the deserted shore lured on a sensitive imagination.

Here I would often lie beside the water, half covered with sand, casting off the burden of my useless thoughts.

AN INDIAN JOURNEY

It was glorious to listen to the voice of the sea which seemed to dominate the world; to watch the ceaseless breaking of the waves, rising first noiselessly like soft breezes rippling a surface of blue silk, and then, with a jubilant crash, throwing themselves in a broad band of light upon the patient strand. The vigil would continue just as long as the mind would give itself up to dreaming, for the sea knows nothing of time. In its voice are neither hopes nor pledges, neither love nor threat, neither prophecies nor assuagements. The nature of the sea has no community with ours, and when we essay to claim kinship with it, nothing comes of it save a sense of exalted discord. It is only its grandeur that uplifts us, for immensity in all its forms affords the spirit a presentment of approaching freedom. The sea offers no measure of our rights and duties as the earth does—the soil that bears and feeds us, the earth whose destiny is akin to our own. Poets have rarely understood the sea—they have merely described it. But who could get from their descriptions, if he had never seen the sea, an image of its immeasurable power and freedom? Only through the soul of the god-intoxicated enthusiast of the Apocalypse shines a prophetic illumination of the essence of the sea, when John in his visions glimpses a new heaven and a new earth, averring that "there was no more sea." Here we discern a profound intuition of its nature—it has never been cursed as earth has been, and therefore knows nothing of judgment, resurrection, or change.

Thus the sea has no kinship with the soul of man, the declamations of those who know neither the one nor the

AN INDIAN JOURNEY

other to the contrary notwithstanding. Because they have an inkling of something fathomless in the soul, they have hit upon the idea that it is perchance as deep as the midmost ocean—a facile conclusion hard to prove. The one true likeness between such intellects and the sea is, that one may often fish in both, with no catch to show for one's pains.

It so chanced once that I found upon the shore a number of large turtles. They were lying on their backs, their mouths gaping for water. Prints of naked feet upon the sand formed a circle round each, making it plain that the beasts had not turned over on their own accord but that there was some human agency at the bottom of their torment. Presently I sighted a brown Hindu boy, flitting away between the trees. He was in such affright at seeing me that he climbed into the crest of a palm.

Deprived of their power of movement, the turtles were doomed to a lingering death in the pitiless rays of the sun —lingering, because these animals do not die quickly out of their element like fish, but cling to life tenaciously upon dry land. Some of them, indeed, were obviously out of sorts. In others, the strange and hideous head was already drooping lifeless at the end of the wrinkled neck, which had the appearance of a cracked indiarubber tube. With considerable effort I turned over those which seemed to be sufficiently alive to have a chance of recovery, but they staggered as if drunk, and did not reach the water until I steered them along. Then they swam off in lively fashion, diving as speedily as possible and plainly doubtful whether to accept their redemption as a fact or an agonised fever-dream of death under the sun rays.

Later on I have been told that the natives capsize the animals that way and leave them to die, for a turtle overturned cannot right itself by its own efforts. This is done to get the much-prized tortoise-shell, without killing the turtles outright which is both forbidden and against their religious tenets. The Hindus consider that the overturned turtles die by the will of the gods and not by any act of man. Since the gods do not assist the turtles to regain their footing, it is their manifest will that they should perish to benefit mankind. Needless to say that I incurred the lasting ill-will of the tortoise-shell handicraftsmen of Cannanore, for the above-mentioned boy, from his lofty coign of vantage, had watched my rescue work and spread the news all over town.

There were crabs of many kinds on the shore and all manner of lesser sea beasts, with whom I made acquaintance. Rats, too, sometimes drifted seawards along the streams to discover whether any dead had been cast up by the sea or disinterred by the waters. One of the Malabar castes buries in the sands of the seashore those who die of the plague. In most cases the interment takes place upon sandbanks and islets, but not infrequently such graves are met with along the coast of the mainland.

On one occasion I encountered a large fly which had only one wing and was apparently destined to spend the rest of its life on shore. I watched it as I lay smoking on the beach. It sought out pebbles which were especially round, white and hot; it seemed to have a preference for

AN INDIAN JOURNEY

white stones. After resting for a time upon one of these, it would take a fancy for another and would endeavour to reach it by a sort of leaping flight. Owing, however, to the loss of its wing, it would not keep a straight course and invariably failed to hit the mark.

Each time it looked round in bewilderment—then submitted to the strange fate which always made it land somewhere else than intended. With a rather troubled but by no means irritated expression, it took stock of its environment. When at length the sunlight reached this stone likewise, the insect remained quiescent in the full glare, in front of the glittering waves.

I took rather a fancy to my chance acquaintance of these lonesome hours on the seashore. After all, I was not much better off, and we both had a passion for the sunlight. I told the fly my mind about existence, and when it paid no heed, I pelted it with tiny pebbles. They rolled over their rounded brothers of the ages with a gay clatter. Most of the stones were beautifully smooth. Picking one up, I took it between my hot hands, polishing it with care.

"You're not round enough yet, my little fellow," I said, and threw it into the sea, so that the waves might rub off its angles for a few thousand years longer. To me a thousand years were but as a day. But perhaps the stone will not forget me. I am sure this must have been the first time that a human ephemerid had taken a personal interest in it, interfering suddenly with its leisurely career.

The sea filled my mind with slight and pleasing thoughts—some were foolish and others pregnant with meaning, but none were grave. The gifts of the sea were dreams, oblivion, slumber. My thoughts rose with the hot, shimmering air into unknown regions, and the fitful ocean breezes wafted them away. People I had known were merged in a luminous universe, through which I moved, as incorporeally as they. Even love became a mere reminiscence.

But never was I troubled with tedium or discontent. Life was a flawless vessel, filled with the clear old wine of a sweet and sensuous joy and a serene love of existence. I came to understand the natives, dwellers in the sunshine, who seemed to have no other motive than the desire to appraise life as a cherished possession, to surrender themselves unreflectingly to the spontaneous play of events, their attitude towards the transient goods of their earthly pilgrimage being one of unselective contentment. What led to quietism and decay in the ignoble, led their nobler kinsfolk to a profound immersion in the clairvoyant humility of self-restraint.

On the shore, between whiles, I paid death a trifle on account and fell asleep; but the voice of the sea went with me into dreamland. In my dreams, the monotony of its level utterance was transmuted into a multiform eloquence, so that through my slumbering brains there passed tales of wonder, sagas of the world's drift that would have filled a volume, had not something of the wisdom of the sea stayed my recording hand.

"My message is the same for everyone," it murmured. "Why make yourself its mouthpiece? Let whosoever will take it firsthand from nature. Since you do not under-

AN INDIAN JOURNEY

stand even yourself, how can you penetrate to my sacred essence?"

I awoke. In the evening glow, upon the silver margin of the waters, I saw close at hand a huge boat rowed by four men standing to their oars and looking quite black against the dazzling background of the sunset sky. Perhaps their goal was distant; perhaps they were homeward bound. I did not know which, in their case any more than in my own.

I have a vivid recollection of a regrettable incident which occurred during this period—one which seriously jeopardised the esteem felt for me by the inhabitants of Cannanore. From earliest childhood I have had an impulse to collect butterflies and beetles, but unfortunately have never had any success in this pursuit. So unlucky have been my endeavours, that it was obvious they were not under a blessing. My parents gave me some magnificent glass cases for the furtherance of my laudable design, but these cases speedily became nothing better than a source of cheap food for tiny louse-like parasites which attacked my collection in myriads, and devoured all the specimens. An experienced schoolfellow recommended me to get some naphthalin, which was, he said, a splendid preservative. But the enemy attacked the naphthalin, ate that also, and seemed to thrive upon it. Thus the results of my labours perished, with the exception of a solitary, reddish sand flea, which was left impaled upon a rusty pin, itself not much larger than the pin's head.

It would certainly have been better had I profited in India by these experiences of childhood's days. Never-

theless, everyone will understand how natural it was that my whilom passion should be revived in full view of the extraordinarily varied and beautiful insect world of Hindustan. I threw Panya's objections to the winds, and had it bruited abroad in Cannanore that I was willing to pay one anna for every butterfly or beetle brought to my house.

The morning after the promulgation of this manifesto, I was awakened quite early by a strange noise outside the house. For a time I could not conceive what was the matter, until at length I realised that I was listening to the murmur of a crowd. In alarm I went to the window, and saw an orderly queue of natives—children, old men, women carrying babies on their hips, men in their prime, lads, and a sprinkling of beggars, prostitutes, and vagabonds. The queue was carefully ranged along the curved garden path; it serpentined through the open gate, and tailed off towards Cannanore. I could not see how long it was. At first I was spared this experience. We know that when fate strikes heavy blows, life often attempts to make things easier for the victim by hiding for a time the full extent of the calamity.

"Sahib, these people are bringing the creatures you asked for," said Panya tartly.

I must admit that I was greatly taken aback. In fact I found it hard to pull myself together; but I made a successful effort, for Panya did not take his eyes from my face and I grudged him the triumph which lurked behind his quiet gaze.

AN INDIAN JOURNEY

"Have you plenty of small change?" I cheerfully enquired, while I dressed as rapidly as possible.

Panya's answer was to ask in all seriousness, whether I had enough money in the house.

Calling Elijah to heel, I donned my sun-helmet, and strode bravely on to the veranda. An approving murmur of expectation greeted me. With a casual air, as if I had no thought beyond taking a turn in the garden, I strolled to the gate, and glanced along the road towards Cannanore. The queue extended farther than I could see, stretching like a charcoal line marked upon the red, laterite road, far onwards beneath the colonnade formed by the banyan trees, until it was lost in the shadows. Elijah slunk into the house, for he had never seen anything like this before. On the veranda, Panya was awaiting me. He had brought out a reclining chair for me to sit upon.

There was nothing left but to begin. Sending Pasha with a handful of rupees to get some change in Cannanore, I employed Panya as dragoman, for had I despatched him to the town he would probably have been all day about his mission, to block my exploit.

The first of the multitude was a small, chubby boy, totally nude, with lovely dark eyes. He boldly held out towards me a tightly closed and exceedingly dirty little fist, and opened to disclose the dusty remnants of a tiny moth, crushed to a pulp. Not wishing to begin with a refusal, I handed him an anna, and the naked little sportsman took his departure with a happy leap, not venturing to utter the shout of jubilation with which he was obviously bursting. It was plain that he had had no faith in the success of his mission. Panya followed the boy with his eyes and said maliciously:

"On the way he will catch one of his own lice, and will take his place once more at the rear of the queue!"

Next came an elderly man, holding in his lean hand a green pouch made out of a great leaf and containing white ants like those with which the house was already swarming. He hoped to receive an anna apiece for these. I waved him away; but he stuck to his plea, and began to relate all the misfortunes of his family, which really seemed to have been rather unlucky. In the end I gave him a couple of annas, and he went away with an ill-favoured glance at the money, after attempting to press on me two of the white ants.

It would take too long to give an account of all the worms, flies, vermin, and multifarious insects, that were brought to me in the course of the morning. There were enough to give me some sort of notion of the wealth of India in this respect. An old woman offered me a chicken which had been half eaten by rats and had no feathers left. She had formed no clear idea of what I was interested in, and hoped I would add this trophy to my collection. A young girl, blooming like the sunlit morning as she shyly stood beside my chair, had a really beautiful butterfly, as large as a warbler, orange in colour, with a delicate lilac border; but she had crushed it between her fingers as a tram ticket may be crushed into a glove. I looked the child over, admiring the natural lustre of her large eyes, which reminded me of dark velvet imbedded in brown silk. Dreams of immemorial antiquity radiated from these eyes,

AN INDIAN JOURNEY

quietly and sadly, like soporific poppy-seed. I experienced a sudden revulsion of feeling. Overcome with melancholy, I realised with a distressing sense of shame the utter futility of my behaviour. How could I have been such a fool as to imagine that we get a hand's breadth nearer to the glories of Nature by putting her products in glass cases? I felt the remorse of one responsible for innumerable murders; and before me stood the army of hired assassins awaiting their reward. I gave the child the rest of the money that Pasha had brought me, and stood up to indicate that my demands were satisfied, and that I did not want any more insects.

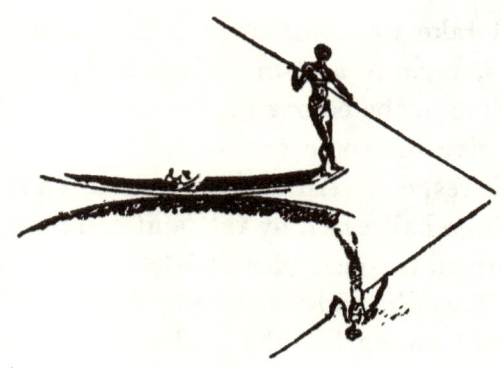

III · A NIGHT WITH HUG, THE MONKEY · III

ONE morning I stepped out on the veranda of my house in Cannanore, to find a brown lad standing there with a monkey perched on his shoulders. There is no telling how long he had been waiting. The natives, including the servants, always hold back modestly until it pleases the sahib to address them; they will stand for hours at a time patiently awaiting his pleasure, even when they think they have already been observed.

It took me many weeks to get used to this.

Once, at the beginning of my journey, in Bijapur, where I had pitched my tent amid the ruins of old imperial castles, I was sitting at my desk late at night, when suddenly I had the impression of some one standing behind me. This sense of an impalpable presence, in the deep of the night, is far more alarming than when you come face to face with a visible opponent. I still remember, vividly, how for a long time I did not dare to move my head, then how, inch by inch I turned around, and started to my feet in sheer fright. There back of me was the outline of a brown figure, dark in dark, like the Evil One himself haunting me. Fortunately, the nocturnal messenger was as violently startled by my alarm as I by his presence, so that I laughed, and the horror was dispelled.

The Hindus catch the sound of bare feet even on cocoanut matting, so that they do not realise, unless they learn by repeated experience, that our ears are accustomed to a more audible approach.

Many foreigners writing about present-day India declare that she has long been shorn of her mystery, her wonder, her secrets. Probably all they know of her are the modern hotels. As for myself, I found the poetic glamour of the Vedas and the spirit of Kalidasa everywhere in the land. Indeed, it was not until I had been in India that I properly understood and revered the Vedas and the spirit of Kalidasa. And while the modern prophets regret their disillusionment, the thing I regret is that it is beyond my powers to give a full, true idea of the mystic glories, the magic of the country.

If you go to India expecting to find the wonder of it in the juggler's art, and are disappointed if you do not get a chance to climb up a rope hanging from the sky, then India will not come up to your expectations. But your disappointment will not be confined to India alone. You will be disappointed wherever you go if you think you can experience something genuine unless you yourself are genuine. The mystical is not the dark or the obscure; it is not the fantastic portent of incomprehensible or mysterious processes. The mystical, in its profoundest sense, involves rather a certitude of eternal truths operating beyond our ken.

Panya explained that the lad waiting on the veranda

AN INDIAN JOURNEY

wanted to sell me his monkey, and expatiated on the advantages of having a monkey in a garden.

"A monkey fetches the cocoanuts down from the palm trees," he said.

The little grey-brown creature on its shoulder-perch, about the size of a fox-terrier, regarded me gravely out of its old features. It was held by a chain attached to a ring round its thin loins. The boy said he was willing to show his monkey off, and the animal actually proved to be remarkably well-trained. The instant it was released from the ring, it rapidly climbed a palm tree, twisted off a nut, let it fall to the ground, descended—more slowly than it had ascended—and patiently let itself be chained again.

Panya bargained with the lad. I did not understand what was being said, but I noticed a look of distress come to the child's face. He seemed to be greedy for the money, and at the same time sad.

"He doesn't want to sell the monkey outright. He just wants to hire it to you," explained Panya. "That's because he's a dunce."

I saw the situation differently. I noted that the child was burning for the sum he had hoped to receive, but that it was hard for him to part forever with his monkey.

"Offer him five rupees," I said.

Panya offered him *one* rupee.

A quiver shook the boy. Even one rupee, which is less than fifty cents, was a treasure to him. His emotion was obviously due to something else besides greed for money. I was interested. I signalled to Panya in a way he could

AN INDIAN JOURNEY

not fail to understand that on this occasion I expected implicit obedience. He knew I understood Canarese well enough to trip him up if he lapsed, and he sank into an attitude of resigned despair, an attitude he always assumed when I went to my ruin regardless of his willingness to serve.

"Why don't you want to sell your monkey?" I asked through my interpreter.

"He's all I have," answered the child.

"But if I give you a big sum of money, you can easily get another. I offer you five rupees."

Panya choked over the words. He had to repeat them.

The child trembled violently. I felt like taking him in my arms.

He spoke hesitatingly.

"There is no monkey like Huc.—Still," he added quickly yet reluctantly, "for such a large sum I will let you have him. You won't beat Huc, or kill him, and if you will let me, I'll come sometimes and look at him through the fence."

"Why do you sell your monkey if you love him?" I asked.

"Shall I really translate such a thing?" asked Panya.

I gave him a look, and he translated like an automaton.

"My parents are starving," said the child, simply, without trace of complaint or accusation.

Then I heard a remarkable story.

The boy's father had been converted to Christianity and had been given a position in a textile factory established by the German mission in Cannanore. While there he had committed several thefts and was discharged. His former associates refused to accept him back in their midst, not because he was a thief, but because he was a renegade. So he was condemned to the life of an outcast, despised in both folds, subjected to the extremes of poverty.

An industrial enterprise cannot, of course, employ thieves. I realised that. Nevertheless various doubts rose to my mind. Was a temple the place for a textile factory? The money-changers and the priests can scarcely bring each other blessing in a House of God; least of all in a Christian House of God.

I was to have more interesting experiences along this line; I was to meet some of these messengers of the Lord and learn to know their nature, their spirit, their value.

Panya, to his distress, now had to make an agreement with the boy, by which I was to have the right to Huc the monkey for two months on the payment of five rupees cash down. The owner was to be allowed to visit his monkey twice a week and was to take him back in case I left Cannanore before the two months were up.

The child hurried home, happy.

And Panya gave me notice. Panya often gave me notice.

As I paid no attention to his threat of resignation, he stood and looked at me.

"Sahib," he began, "you'll be ruined. In a few weeks you'll be ruined. And then where will I be, and my old mother, and my brothers and sisters, and my mother's sisters, and the rice-fields on the Purrha?"

"Panya," I replied politely, "a few weeks ago, when I

paid you the tenth rupee in advance, you told me your mother had died and you had to have the money for her funeral."

"My grandmother," said Panya. "Shall I tell you about her?"

"Your grandmother died when we arrived in Bijapur."

"You are mixing everything up," said Panya gloomily. "The only thing you seem able to remember accurately is the amount of the advance."

I felt that this limited praise of my memory was unmerited, for Panya's advance was twice as large as I had ventured to state, and I resolved to be more straightforward in future.

When I returned from the seashore in the evening, after buying a boat in the fishing village, I found Huc in my room. Panya had vanished, and Pasha silently served my dinner on the veranda. I watched his movements, and his imperturbable demeanour. He took the earthenware pitcher containing boiled water out of the bamboo cradle in which it had been hanging to get cool; brought the made dishes and the fruit in serious and careful fashion. All the things were in separate little dishes, tastefully arranged —custard-apples, ginger, roasted bananas, and rice with curry and cocoanut milk. Long ere this I had accustomed myself to the Indian diet, which few are privileged to know thoroughly in its great diversity, for even in native hotels the Hindus try to supply European guests with food prepared after the European manner. But anyone who has learned the wealth of India in fruits, and who under-

AN INDIAN JOURNEY

stands how to adapt the various kinds to his needs, will fare sumptuously. He will prefer this refreshing and wholesome diet to any other, and will never forget his enjoyment of it.

When Pasha was bringing the pineapple, the bananas, and the early mangoes (which generally speaking were not yet ripe in Malabar), he saw Huc the monkey sitting on the table among the dishes and was shocked.

"I will take him away," said Pasha.

But I explained that I wished to talk to Huc, so the cook departed in silence. At first the monkey had had scant confidence in me, and had timidly withdrawn from my advances. After a while, however, he made up his mind that I meant him no harm. Thereupon, contemplating me with comparative indifference, he rather hesitatingly accepted with a limp paw whatever I offered him. The poor beast was extremely mistrustful of human beings, for the lot of a captive monkey in India is seldom a happy one. He has to suffer for all the hatred and contempt incurred by his thievish fellow-monkeys. Every passer-by seems to take a delight in working off on the prisoner some of the anger that the free monkeys, safe in the crowns of the palm trees, have aroused by their impudence. But the captive monkey's worst troubles come from children, for in respect of thoughtless cruelty the children of India are not to be outdone by those of any other land. Perverse traits manifest themselves in early years; and what is a monkey's life worth in India, where human life is held so cheap? The lad who had brought

AN INDIAN JOURNEY

Huc to me was exceptional in his attitude towards the animal.

The evening sun was still shining. I had had a narrow clearing cut through the palm grove, to open a view to the coast; but now I could only see the plateau behind which the ocean was breathing, could enjoy its cool exhalation, and hear its muffled drumming on the rocks. On the top of the plateau were visible the silhouettes of two palms, one of which rose straight and stiff like a candle, while the other leaned gracefully to one side. Against the red glow of the evening sky, the stems were like black lines delicately traced with charcoal. They rose on the music of the sea, midway towards the freedom of the heavens on which my eyes dwelt evening after evening during my stay in Cannanore. Long after I had left the neighbourhood, I had merely to close my eyes to revive this picture, and with it the half-forgotten images of my life in India, whose splendours no mortal tongue can tell. Amid the busy hum of European cities, in the turmoil of the streets, in brightly lighted halls among chattering and laughing men and women, or in the lonely calm of my study at night, I sometimes see this simple picture, and with it there recurs the sublime melody of the ocean and the greeting of the water to the dusky rocks. Therewith comes an unquenchable yearning for the East, and a feeling of supreme peace.

Night fell. Huc obviously wished to stay with me, and I had no objection, for I had a strange and oppressive feeling that he and I had a great deal to say to one another. More than all other living creatures, the monkey arouses

AN INDIAN JOURNEY

in us an inclination to meditate upon ourselves. As, to cheer my loneliness, I slowly drank glass after glass of the heavy Indian palm-wine, dream figures, crowned with vine leaves, danced before my eyes. Gradually the forces of everyday life lost their sway over my mind, being replaced by better and higher energies which can give no material token of their power. Throughout this time, Huc sat before me, quietly meditating, and watching me patiently. His remarkably delicate, light-grey eyelids, which resembled thin guttapercha, were seldom raised more than to disclose the halves of his weary eyes. His dun-coloured hands, with pigmented nails, and wrinkled like the hands of an old man, led a sleepy life of their own, of which his thoughts seemed to take no account.

"Huc," I said, "my borrowed monkey, the gait of the human heart, when in solitude it commits itself to the winged promptings of wine, is the same all over the world. There are differences in degree, but the kind is as universal as human fellowship, which is shared by all who accept the blessings of a sacrament. Do we not feel at first as if the cares of everyday life had quietly withdrawn, so that, astonished and greatly delighted, we seek to discover what has put them to flight? Upon the battlefield of our painful sojourn, a battlefield now verdant once again, arises the kindly angel of hope. This angel, without blinding our eyes, with imposing mien makes the most beautiful possibilities of our future a certainty for us, so that imperceptibly we find ourselves at the goal of our desires. But thus it comes to pass with us, Huc, that at this goal we grow melancholy of a sudden. To the sort of

AN INDIAN JOURNEY

good fellow that wine produces it is disagreeable to have no desires; and for this reason the goal we have attained proves to be nothing more than the outlook towards a new one. With the premonition, at once painful and joyful, that this will always be so, there awakens in our heart the yearning for a permanent good."

"Don't you wish you may get it?" interjected Huc.

"You must not interrupt," I exhorted, feeling that annoyance which is usual in persons who fancy their thoughts to be far more important than they really are, and who therefore imagine that those who fail to share their feelings wish to create a diversion. "Huc, we must now discover where this desideratum lies hid, and under what guise it stalks abroad. It emerges from the dregs of our glass, from the shadow of the cup, and assumes the likeness of a woman reflected in its golden mirror.

> "Whatever we believe in,
> Radiates from the bottom of the cup:
> The drooping head of Christ,
> Or the beloved one's mouth."

"No poetry, please," said Huc.

"I'm sorry," I answered. "Verses come into one's head unawares; but of course I know how few people understand that only in verse can things be said really well. Don't you notice, Huc, that the likeness of this woman resembles none of the things with which we are familiar? The beauty and gentleness of her face are unknown on earth, and therein lies her ineffable power of consolation. Her eyes radiate imperishable life and the sleep of mortals: out of sleep there arise lovely veils, as the odour of jasmine

AN INDIAN JOURNEY

rises on a summer night; with these veils our eyes are covered, so that we sink into repose as if we had desired nothing in the world beyond this grateful rest."

"It seems that the only reason why you are an ascetic," responded Huc, "is because on the road thither you can enjoy a number of agreeable sensations." He brushed his hand swiftly across the thin lips of his wide mouth, which looked like a slit cut in a dark hemisphere; then, raising his eyebrows, he let his hand fall absently. "Give me a drink," he went on, thrusting up his shoulders, so that his head pushed forwards between them and looked as large as a man's. He drank cautiously, licked his lips composedly, and sighed just like a human being.

Silence prevailed for a time, broken only by the hushed sounds of the night without, and by the gentle and mysterious murmur of the earth on its journey. Then Huc laid his soft hand on his heart, and said simply:

"I am consumptive, and have not long to live. Let me tell you about the forests. I have not much to say, for they are so beautiful that thoughts and words about them seem more like dreams the nearer they are to truth. Do not imagine that my illness disturbs me. None but the poor-spirited are troubled about their bodies. Physical pain and bodily weakness should be greeted with a smile."

"Your wisdom astonishes me, Huc," said I.

"How arrogant you must be to be astonished," replied Huc calmly. "You men have forgotten how to honour the creator in the living essence of creation; and you overestimate your own merits so greatly that you are contemptuous of the merits of other creatures. But we are

AN INDIAN JOURNEY

upon the same road, every one of us. If we were intelligent enough to understand time, if we could contemplate both the past and the future, we should be more reverent, more modest, and more pious. Give me another drink."

I handed him the glass, which he held in both hands as he slowly drained it with closed eyes.

"All good men like to study the behaviour of animals," continued Huc tranquilly. "It rouses to emotion and vague belief their anticipations of a future state of perfection. Some of you are a stage advanced, and have learned to admire the qualities of plants, which are no less diversified in themselves although they differ from the qualities of animals. But when will you study the life of stones? Human beings have lost patience. I have had to live among them for a long time, and in doing so have not merely suffered (as you supposed when you borrowed me), but have also learned. I have made acquaintance with their houses and their towns; I have journeyed down the coast in a ship from which the forests along the shore looked like fine, blue clouds; I have even travelled by rail, so that I know the things men are proud of. From human companions I have contracted my disease, for in the rain and the wind and the scorching sun I was left unprotected on the post to which I was chained. You will be the last of my masters. Drink up!"

I fetched another glass for myself, and filled for us both. Huc sat in front of me on the table between two bottles glittering in the candlelight, looking at me out of his elderly, thoughtful eyes. He sat so that our foreheads were on a level. The monkey played for a time with a

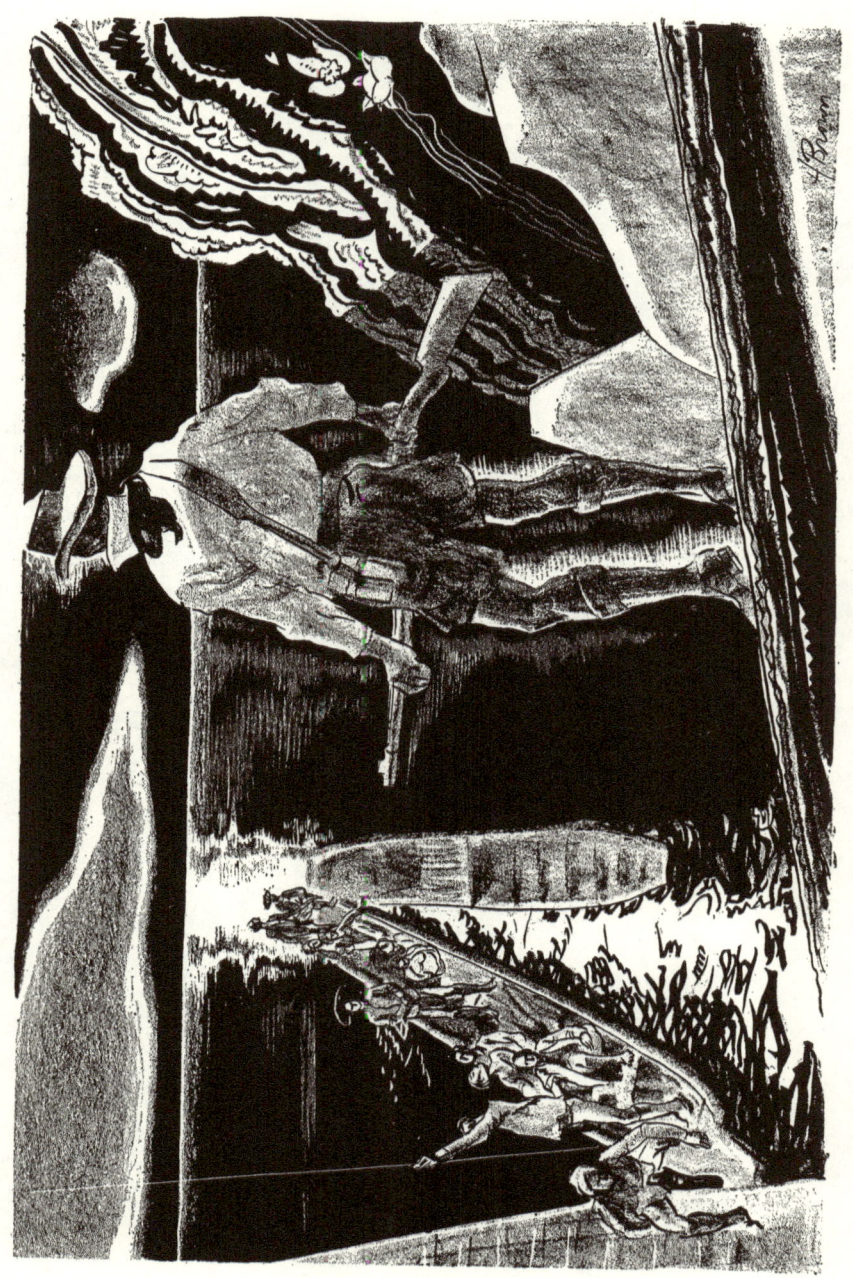

AN INDIAN JOURNEY

piece of coloured tinfoil, tore it asunder, and smelt the fragments. When, at length, he dropped them as if he had never had the slightest interest in them, I was again puzzled for a moment as to his meaning.

"After all, you are only a monkey," I said, as if awakening from a dream.

Huc drew his long tail pensively through his hand, gripped it by the end, and enquired, thrusting his round muzzle towards me:

"How much have you had to drink by now?"

I begged his pardon shamefacedly. Huc had really been right, as I had realised at the time, when from his young master's shoulder he had contemplated me with his imperturbable seriousness and his fathomless sense of superiority.

"Please tell me about the forest," I said.

"I often think," began Huc in a quiet tone, "that I have first come to know the forests since I was compelled to leave them, for since that day, hour by hour, they have been ever in my dreams. This has taught me that what we love does not seem really to belong to us until we have lost it. With everything petty dropped in the rear, I beheld one radiant picture of glorious freedom. This alone remains in my memory: interwoven with the white splendour of the moonlight over the leafy canopy; with the play of the sunbeams amid the fresh, green foliage; with the song of the nightingale beside the stream; and with the scent of the flowers, more varied in form and tint than fancy can picture. You will outlive me, so I will leave you a yearning for the forests as a legacy in safe keeping."

AN INDIAN JOURNEY

In token of assent, I raised my glass to drain it anew, but Huc did not drink with me. He snuggled up against one of the bottles (it was almost as large as himself), as if its motley sparkles in the candlelight could warm him. Monotonously he continued, unmoved as it seemed, for he neither smiled nor showed any sign of regret:

"I was taken captive one morning in spring. My home is a long way from here, in the jungles of Mangalore, the ancient seaport. In one of the rice-fields I was caught in a snare set by human hands. When I realised that I could not break the hempen cord round my arms and shoulders, I resigned myself to my fate. Two boys carried me off to a poor hut, built of mud and palm leaves between the hanging roots of a banyan tree. It stank of sandalwood and burnt cow dung, and was so dark and stuffy that for a long time I was bewildered. When I awoke in the morning after my first night, I saw the banana leaves in the sunshine in front of the tiny window, and my thoughts turned to my companions. Now, like myself formerly, they were swinging in the morning breeze upon the crests of the areca palms; they were watching the cranes as the birds stood fishing in shallow water upon sandbanks in the river. When I closed my eyes, I could hear the whispering of the water and the rustle of the wind among the reeds. I could hear the love-song of the wild doves in the thicket. I could see the panther creeping among the sedges on his way down to drink. As he moved through the strips of sunlight and shadow in the reed-bed, it seemed as if sun and wind were playing with sunlight and shadow, and no one would have spied him had he not betrayed himself by raucous snarling, or by his steaming breath, heavy with the halitus of his last kill. From on high came the clear call of the kite, circling on the watch for prey. Goldspangled looked the bird as he hovered, small and happy in the cool heights over the wild green sea of the jungle. I was rubbing shoulders with my companions among the tree-tops in the red light of dawn, breathing the fresh air, and sensing the silent movements of the countless plants below me as they stretched sunwards. Could you have lived with me in the primeval forest, you would have learned to hear the sweet and passionate murmur of the opening flowers; you would have become able to distinguish the aroma of the bursting bud from the stronger scent of the full-blown flower; and you would be familiar with the voluptuous urge, the eager germination, and the rapture, of these patient ones in the impulsive need of their springtime ecstasy.

"But to your human kind, the commonplace is all-important; and trivialities are more highly esteemed by men than a contemplative communion with the life of nature. You regard us monkeys as a useless and empty-headed tribe, which does nothing worth doing, and fritters away its days. How little you know of the happiness of our free life under the sun, or when the moon shines in the white and teeming night. How little you know of our kinship with the blameless destinies of the manifold creatures of nature. Can you not realise that we would not exchange an hour of peaceful communion with the happy ones of the forest, for all the tawdry trifles with which you crowd your fevered days? The fact that our qualities differ from yours does not shut us out from earthly happiness; and are your temporal aims anything else than the pursuit of happiness? You make mock of us because we enjoy our freedom—forgetting that without freedom we are nothing. Only in happiness can we really learn to know anything; for happiness is essential to a well-considered knowledge of self, and out of self-knowledge comes all that is great."

"What great things have ever come from monkeys?" I enquired.

Huc shrugged his shoulders. His face became grey and old, as if he had lived thousands of years. It recalled that of a mummy; and had at the same time a melancholy, animal-like expression, indescribable in its menacing earnestness.

"Only a human being could ask such a question," said he, dryly. "You always think that you can improve upon nature, and imagine that you cannot go on existing unless you create something. Your continued existence has nothing to do with your activities; and as long as you believe that you can find salvation in struggle, you are merely showing that you do not know what salvation is. The greatness which arises out of true self-knowledge is not the work of human hands, but is love for all created nature."

"What do you know of God, monkey?" said I.

"All that matters is that God should know something of me," answered Huc; "and he does. Those only are unhappy whom God has forgotten."

"True, Huc, true. I did you an injustice."

"Now you are actually beginning to believe me," re-

AN INDIAN JOURNEY

joined the monkey, with a gloomy air. "Nothing else could make me doubt whether I am right."

It seemed that Huc had a very poor opinion of me. I do not know how I had incurred his displeasure. Perhaps it was because I had drunk too much palm-wine.

"Go on telling me about the forests," I implored. "Don't let us argue about God. No wise man argues about God."

"That is an excellent reason why you should do it," retorted Huc. He opened his mouth a little, so that I saw his teeth gleam, and suddenly I fancied that a terrible malice lurked behind his features.

I was overcome by an intolerable sense of anger. The main cause, doubtless, was not so much the monkey's secret scorn, as the almost frenzied feeling of shame that possesses us when we perceive that the edifice of a false notion of God is collapsing under the impact of an elemental love of nature. Beside myself with wrath, I seized one of the bottles by the neck, swung it high in the air, and brought it down with a crash on Huc's bald head. The fragments scattered in all directions in a many-coloured rain, and as I opened eyes that were blinded by a shaft of light, I seemed to see a dark shadow slink away.

I realised that the morning sun was shining on the leaves, and that I had gone to sleep seated at the table with my head pillowed on my arms. Bemused and numb, I looked around me, for the clink of broken glass still rang so plainly in my ears that I felt sure I must have smashed one of the bottles. Then I saw that in my sleep I had pushed a glass off the table. On the floor, the shivers glittered in the morning light. A cool breeze blew through the half-opened window, bearing with it the cry of the parakeets from the mango trees. I stretched my stiffened limbs, and yawned over the lake of wine on the table, in which my cigar had been drowned. Still somewhat confused, I at length collected myself sufficiently to look for Huc's corpse, but the monkey was nowhere to be seen. Then, as I caught sight of the open window, I was seized with alarm as I realised what must have happened to Huc. With a certain sense that the weakness of age was upon me, walking very straight and swinging my arms rather freely, I went on to the veranda, and caught sight of Huc upon the crown of a palm tree. He looked as if he were sitting on his hands, and was rocking to and fro in delight. When I called him, he looked down, shrugged his shoulders, and showed his teeth as though laughing at me. Soon, however, he ceased to take any interest in me. He blinked at the morning sun, let the branch on which he was sitting sway as it pleased, inclined his clever little manlike head to one side, and closed his eyes for very joy of life.

When I re-entered the room, Panya was standing in the open doorway, with his hands clasped behind him. He had the fresh look of one who has slept well. His coal-black hair was surmounted by a clean turban. His eyes wandered from the overturned wine bottle, now to the shivers of glass on the floor, and now to my own figure as I stood there in poor case, stale after a debauch.

"Sahib . . ." he said, and put his arms akimbo.

I will make no attempt to describe his face, which is not

a pleasant memory. Now, I thought, he will ask what has become of the monkey—but he did nothing of the kind. Since the night when he had found Elijah alone in my bed, Panya had been convinced that I was past aiding. With a most offensive air of superiority which I mentally scored up against him, he announced:

"Sahib, a fisherman has come to tell you that there is an east wind, and that your boat is ready to put to sea."

IV · · VALARPATTANAM LAGOON · · IV

DAY by day the weather grew hotter. At midday I fell asleep over my cigar in the hammock, to awaken depressed and lethargic. Even my books would lie upon the writing table for days, open at the same page. I was still determined to travel, so I studied the very inadequate maps, having already made up my mind to journey northwards across the river mouths, although the streams were still in flood and the country was under water in places. The officers of the British garrison, with some of whom I had now become acquainted, advised me against this plan. But they did not understand my object. Of course they would have been right had my sole intent been to cover the ground quickly and conveniently. However, in about a fortnight, I had made all necessary preparations. I had hired a bullock cart, laid in stores sufficient for two months, and one morning a lad came to tell me that the boats were ready for us at Beliapatam.

The Valarpattanam (or Beliapatam) and the Ponnani are the two largest rivers of Malabar, lying respectively

in the north and the south of the region. Like most of
the rivers of the west coast, just before it reaches the sea,
the Valarpattanam forms a basin of considerable size, with
a narrow outlet through which the tide ebbs and flows.
These lagoons of the individual rivers are connected by
means of canals. Before the struggles of the English with
Tipu Sahib, that ruler, as far-seeing as he was cruel, had
had these canals made, so that trade between the coast
towns need not be interrupted by the monsoon, when the
storms rendered coastal navigation impracticable. To-
day, when traffic along the coast is mainly carried on in
steamships, this magnificent waterway across the lagoons
and through the primeval forest has been almost forgotten.
The canals have become partly silted up during the floods
of successive rainy seasons and in places they have been
completely overgrown by the luxuriant vegetation.

Panya was in high spirits now that I had announced my
intention to leave the town. He did not like Cannanore,
and preferred to be with me in places where we ruled as
monarchs. When he was informed of my chosen route, he
scratched his neck joyfully and meditatively, casting a
sidelong glance at me. I feel sure, now, that he had a
good notion of what was in store for us, and was chuckling
to himself at the prospect that I should soon be entirely
dependent upon his aid. He conducted the preparations
with considerable skill, and by degrees some of the ar-
rangements which he resolutely undertook on his own ini-
tiative made me aware of the difficulties with which we
should have to cope. He exchanged the last of my leather
trunks for a tin box, and a number of these metal cases

AN INDIAN JOURNEY

disappeared into the baggage cart. He advised me not to wear my revolver openly, but to go armed, since we were to have Mohammedan boatmen.

I did not know to what extent his fears were justified, but I knew that the less desirable elements of the Hindu world become converts to Islam simply to enjoy the larger freedom open to those who profess that creed. In the western provinces, the Mohammedans form an aloof and resolute community. They are more dangerous to the English than the Hindus, for the latter are split up into a hundred and one different castes and therefore lack solidarity of interest.

Speaking generally, our equipment emphasised rather the peacefulness than the dangers of the country. The dangers of India do not come from human beings. I recalled, in comparison, what I had seen of the preparations for another pilgrimage into the wilderness, a journey through Soudan. On that occasion the motley camp was littered with weapons and death-dealing instruments; the shining forms of the huge negroes inspired the observer with a secret dread of their savage brethren in the interior; and when the vultures were soaring above the place from which the expedition was to start, one could hear in fancy the wings of the Angel of Death whose terrible countenance seemed to eradiate the plagues of Africa and the bloodthirstiness of febrile paroxysms. Long afterwards, when I had been back in Europe for a considerable time, I learned that not one of that company ever found his way home. The last survivor perished in a Genoese hospital. A penniless beggar, fever-stricken and eaten up by a loathsome disease, he had landed at Naples and was trying to make his way back to Germany on foot.

The perils of India, on the other hand, have little to do with the indigenous population, for the inhabitants are peaceful and kindly, show no lust for slaughter, and have for thousands of years been subject to strict rule. Apart from the passions fomented by political fanaticism and from the crimes resulting from revenge, hatred, and the craving for power, in the greater part of the peninsula European travellers are in no danger from the natives. Were it not for the risks of fever, wild beasts, and plague, modern India would be far less dangerous than the outskirts of a great European city at night. The perils of India, its influences, and its secret powers, belong to a latitude of existence very different from that in which knife or pistol is decisive for weal or woe. India offers few dangers to anyone whose demands do not go beyond the preservation of his transitory life; but the dæmonic spirit of India touches the very marrow of the soul where it is endeavouring to solve the great problems of existence and to storm the heights of human consciousness. With the incomprehensible tranquillity of its heavenly triumph, the ancient spirit of the eternal realm of God paralyses all the fierce zeal of struggle and research, all youth fighting for knowledge, and the vigour of all spiritual activity. What is, has been.

> Understanding performs the sacrifice,
> It performs all sacred acts.
> All Devas worship understanding
> As Brahman, as the oldest.

AN INDIAN JOURNEY

*If a man has understanding as Brahman,
And if he does not swerve from it,
He leaves all evil behind in the body,
And attains all his wishes.*

To the heavenly worlds of the Upanishad and to its light, no spiritual ray is alien which turns towards them from the realm of our civilisations. The only alternatives are, the contemplative life with its submission and tranquillity, or perpetual revolution. Throughout India, the peace of the Upanishad broods over the living and the dead. An old proverb says that he who enters India without patience will soon learn it, but that he who comes to this land armed with patience will lose it. If we apply the saying merely to externals, it may seem to have a trifling and anecdotal significance; but in its inner meaning it bears upon the ancient spiritual essence of the millenniums which is dominant throughout Hindustan. By the roadside in the peninsula sits the spirit of mankind with grey hair and youthful eyes; sits with a quiet smile of triumph, contemplating the ashes of the vanished generations and the foolish activities of those who still crowd the scene. No one whose conscience is uneasy with the timeworn conviction of sin, will pass the spirit unheeded; but children do not see it—nor pharisees with their pitiable self-satisfaction.

Doubtless one of the main causes which impelled me to a communing with virgin nature, the mother of faith and charity for all candid souls, was my strange dream of Huc the monkey. Who can decide whether our dreams are capable of starting trains of thought, as it were in an innocent automatism of the brain which resembles a miraculous revelation; or whether our waking thoughts initiate our dreams? It seemed to me at that time as if a new philosophical evangel was to be found in Huc's simple statement that the great things of our earthly life can come to us only out of our love for all the creations of nature. Another of his phrases that still ran in my mind was: "Your continued existence has nothing to do with your activities; and as long as you believe that you can find salvation in struggle, you are merely showing that you do not know what salvation is."

Such were the thoughts that inspired my restlessness. They inspired my search for the heart of the ancient realm: in the rippling of the streams and the rustling of the leaves; in the blue heavens over the wilderness of the jungle; in the behaviour of the creatures of India, whether men, beasts, or plants; and in the superabundance of sunshine that pours down over the movement of the ages and over the patient recurrence, which seem, in intimate union, to have given birth to Brahmin as their highest aspiration and ultimate fulfilment.

I was driven by the happy errors of my youth; as millions before me have been uplifted or debased, freed or fettered, blest or corrupted or destroyed, but never granted full satisfaction. Yet their bodies germinate as the resurrections of nature, transformed into new hope and new faith. They become bubbling springs; swelling fruits; or the songs of birds which, interwoven with light-waves, sound over the bursting blossoms. Krishna's great words concerning his own nature—the refulgence of the supreme

AN INDIAN JOURNEY

godhead—lure and guide us ever anew in the unending search for consummation within ourselves.

> I am the goal, the sustainer, the lord, the supervisor,
> The residence, the asylum, the friend,
> The source, and that in which it merges,
> The support, the receptacle, and the inexhaustible seed.

When our bullock cart left Cannanore on its northward journey, the Hindus, newly awakened, and shivering in the cool of the morning, were still standing in the entries of their huts. It was wonderfully fresh. The daily round of human life had scarcely begun. Nothing greeted us but the song of the birds, the morning light flashing from the dew—the light red-tinted on the broad highway, splashed with green and brown from the palms and the undergrowth.

I cast no backward glances. The eager delight of expectation was struggling with the subdued melancholy of parting. This dejection did not amount to pain; it was no more than the sadness of those who, inspired with a thousand new hopes, abandon an old love while still cherishing it. The mail cart from the hill station of Dindimal met us, and passed like a whirlwind, to the accompaniment of a flourish on the horn. Four native ponies, galloping helter-skelter, sweated beneath the noisy whip-lashing of the driver, who squatted on the box gibbering like an angry ape as he flogged them. The overloaded cart rattled and bounded along behind the team. There was no room left in it even for a mouse. In the very window frames and upon the crazy roof, partially naked Indians were crouching upon bundles and boxes, clinging to one another, and

AN INDIAN JOURNEY

raising a clamour which was half excitement and jubilation and half fear. No one knew what reason there was for this terrible speed, which endangered the lives of all the passengers. The urgency of the mission was ascribed to the inscrutable wisdom of the authorities, whose Eurasian representatives were still sound asleep in Cannanore. This storm of noise and folly vanished down the road in a cloud of red dust.

Panya, who was sitting on the shaft beside the driver and owner of the bullock cart, turned towards me, pushed aside the bamboo screen, and expressed his sentiments pithily. He uttered only two words, "Wild pigs," and let the screen fall back into its place. Peace was restored, the sun rose higher, the wheels groaned, and from the rice-fields below the road came the call of the jay-thrush with its three melodious flute-like notes.

After a time we left the posting road and turned into a narrow by-road which ran an open course between freshly irrigated rice-fields, for it had no bordering of trees. The small, white oxen stepped out briskly so that our pace was almost equal to that of a slowly trotting horse. In the southern parts of India, oxen are a far more trustworthy means of transport than horses, for they stand the heat better and are less fastidious as to diet. As the day advanced, I became full of the cheerfulness natural to those who are young and care-free when they start on a journey. Most people are better when travelling than amid the petty vexations of the narrow life of home. With my memories of my years of travel, which filled almost all the time of my early manhood, is associated the feeling that I was then a far better man than I am to-day. Travelling chastens the spirit, for new surroundings make us modest—though not modest in the sense of open-mouthed admiration. Respect for foreign things, for which we Germans are often reproached, is only a fault when it is accompanied by a sacrifice of our own essential nature. But respect for foreign thoughts and actions, and for modes of life that differ from our own, serves in all richly endowed temperaments to subdue the tendency to the carping criticism and excessive self-esteem which are the crying sins of our younger generation.

I do not mean to imply that my mind was then filled with these thoughts. Such ideas come subsequently; they are purposeless for the most part, and serve none but persons who do not really need them. Good ideas are properly understood by those only whose merit it is that they have ideas of their own. At the moment of which I am writing, I was solely concerned with the glorious clearness of the morning, with the peaceful life of the fertile rice-fields, with the rhythmical beat of the water-mills, and with the shapely figures of the men and women at their labours. By degrees the country grew wilder. Once only, when our cart emerged into the open from an arcade formed by tall bushes and overarching foliage, there came an expanse of dark ploughland which had not yet been flooded, and the oblique rays of the sun threw the furrows into a relief of light and shade. The freshness of morning radiated abundantly over the land teeming with fruitfulness. A young man was driving two milk-white oxen yoked to the bent piece of wood which in India serves for a

AN INDIAN JOURNEY

plough. His body was bare save for a loin-cloth, and his long black hair was crowned by a bright red turban. The background to this picture was formed by a palm grove, surmounted by the limitless expanse of the clear blue sky.

At the other end of the field, two girls were working at a water-mill. Perhaps fourteen or fifteen years old, they were almost nude, and their raven hair, shining with oil, hung in a long narrow coil over the light brown neck. They were busily occupied; their virgin bodies moved with the still uncomprehended felicity of youthful freedom; over their work they sang in unison a sad and monotonous air. Amid the noise of the water-mill and of their own voices, they did not for some time note the approach of the bullock cart. When at length they spied us, they leapt across the little brook like startled antelopes, and with a loud outcry took refuge behind the reed walls of a little hut. From out this hut there now came a shrunken old woman, whose withered countenance beamed at us as she nodded a greeting. Then the woodland closed in once more, and grew denser and denser. Here the sunlight only reached us in isolated shafts; it was dark and sultry; more and ever more our outlook into the shadows of the virgin forest was hindered by the bamboo undergrowth and the network of interwoven lianas.

No one was more delighted, to begin with, at the drift of our journey, than Elijah. In the first hour, he must have covered the distance traversed by the cart at least ten times over; in the second hour, he multiplied the journey about five times; even during the third hour, when it had already grown extremely hot, he continued to run gaily to and fro, excelling us all in zeal and staying-power. But when we entered the forest, he grew thoughtful. From time to time, taken aback, he would stand at gaze, endeavouring to pierce the twilit recesses between the tree stems, usually in the attitude of a pointer. His ears were continually at work. Occasionally he would look at me enquiringly as if uncertain whether I found this new demesne as awesome as he did.

I should mention that Elijah's development had gone on apace. He now displayed clearly the characters of a wolf-dog and sheep-dog, in conjunction with those of a stout and active terrier of a breed then popular among the English. His woolly hair was the delight even of connoisseurs owing to its thickness and its many shades of colour. A specially fine ornament was his large, curly tail. As he had now grown to a considerable size, the gentle charm of his appearance had to some extent been replaced by threatening characteristics, of which he failed to take due advantage owing to the excellence of his temper. There can be no doubt that he had a good deal of sporting-dog blood in his veins; for directly a wing stirred, Elijah was possessed with an irresistible desire to get hold of the bird and tear it to pieces. In this respect he showed a praiseworthy courage, which it would not be easy to match.

A glorious time now began! How shall I describe the radiant clearness of the early mornings, the glowing heat of the tranquil days, and the lambent whiteness of the peaceful yet danger-fraught nights? Of all my experience in these wanderings through the wilderness, that which is

AN INDIAN JOURNEY

most indelibly printed on my memory and which I love most to recall is the boat journey along the canals and across the lagoons. Never shall I forget the evening hour when our cart reached the little port of Beliapatam, on the shore of the lagoon into which the Valarpattanam expands just before reaching the sea. The place nestled among palm trees; and, as we drove down to the shore of the lagoon, the white, brown, and green tints contrasted strangely with the greyish-blue, silvery expanse of water. Blue smoke rose from the squat houses and palm-leaf huts, and the chanting of priests came to our ears from the shadowy interior of a wooden pagoda. Not a breath stirred the air, for the stillness of the hot hours lingered, and the waters of the lagoon were unruffled. Huge leafy trees resembling maples shaded the narrow dock in which the boats were lying, closely packed, as if inlaid in metal, many of them piled high with bales of vivid colours. The roads leading to this dock were lined with houses, and from these were wafted odours of tea, spices, and fruits. When the cart halted at the waterside, a white-robed elder arose and greeted us in the name of Allah and the Prophet.

"Are you the lord who wishes to travel to Taliparamba by water?"

He wore a white turban low on the brow, and his dark eyes contemplated me with a meditative steadfastness as he said:

"Give me the money for the journey, Sahib; we must pay the oarsmen in advance, to make sure of their obedience."

Panya pushed in between us, deliberately jostling the

AN INDIAN JOURNEY

old man, and forcing him to step back. The Moslem looked fiercely at the boy.

"Who gave you permission to address the Sahib?" hissed Panya. I was astounded at his impudence. "Step aside. Let us see your boats, so that the Sahib may learn if they are good enough. Do you think he came here to waste his time talking to such as you?"

The old man hesitated, looking towards me doubtfully. Then he followed Panya, and said falteringly:

"The boats are good."

"That is for me to decide," returned Panya coldly.

"Is it a great lord whom you are guiding through the country?" enquired the elder.

Panya laughed contemptuously. "You people of Beliapatam are as ignorant as the frogs in your marshes. The Collector of Mangalore eagerly awaits his arrival, and is sending one messenger after another to know when he is coming. Have you had no messenger?"

The elder shook his head, and looked at me timidly. I was pleased with Panya, since, for all his tendency to show off, I knew that on this occasion he had good reason for what he did. I had often been warned about the Mohammedans, and Panya knew his own country. We examined the boats carefully. They were dug-outs, about twenty-five feet in length, hollowed tree trunks with long outriggers, for the oarsmen stood to their work. There was a well-made linen awning over the middle, arched and tightly stretched, resembling the tilt used on wagons in Germany. Between the roof and the edge of the boat was a narrow space through which the passengers could

AN INDIAN JOURNEY

look out. In front of this cabin was an unroofed platform about six feet long, for use in the cooler hours of the day when it was not necessary to seek shelter from the sun. The floor was covered with clean bamboo matting and with a number of cushions. The boats were very narrow, no wider than a camp bed.

Panya was satisfied. I gazed across the lagoon, which was assuming a reddish tint.

"When does the moon rise?" asked Panya.

"Towards midnight," replied the elder, after a moment's reflection. "We can start at dawn."

"Who is the traveller?" enquired Panya imperturbably. "You or the Sahib? We must start at once."

"Impossible! The people of Beliapatam are away at work, and cannot be gathered in a moment."

Panya ignored the objection and asked:

"How many oarsmen are needed?"

"Four for each boat."

"Two will suffice," insisted Panya. "The water is calm."

The elder dissented. "To-morrow you will be in the open sea, though only for a short time. Two oarsmen cannot manage the boat in the surf."

The elder, it seemed, was right in this particular, for Panya gave way; but he stuck to his point that the oarsmen were to be summoned without delay, and assigned to their respective boats. He explained to me subsequently that it was better for the oarsmen to have no opportunity of exchanging opinions concerning us before the start. Panya had his way. Our baggage was transferred to the boats, and the bullock cart started on its homeward journey that very night. In little more than an hour, we set off under the starlight.

I was awakened by the chant of the oarsmen. Had I really been asleep? It took me a little time to collect my thoughts. The cool night air had an unfamiliar scent. I heard the ripple of the water, and sat up drowsily.

The stars were scintillating as I crept out of the cabin. Beneath me they sank into fathomless abysses, motionless, without a twinkle, looking like diamonds on coal-black silk. Between two sparkling hemispheres, the sky and its reflection, dark and naked bodies were swaying, intercepting the light of the stars in the sky and the images in the water. The oars dipped, and then rose as if from molten silver, as the water flowed sparkling and glittering over the blades. When I turned to look backwards, I saw in our wake a narrow, silvery track, so dazzling in its refulgence that my eyes were well-nigh blinded.

Like a comet with a long tail, the boat was hastening through a shoreless universe glittering with heavenly sparks. Nowhere could I make out any land. We were in the middle of the lagoon, this expansion of the sluggish stream, slowly moving seawards over the ooze that had been forming through the ages. I dipped my hand into the water, and instantly it was enchased in silver. Overpowered by emotion, made giddy by the wonders of the night, I leaned motionless against the awning. Towards midnight, bluish pinnacles of cloud made their appearance in the light of the rising moon, which showed above the jungle like an ochre-tinted sickle. Now we were close to the shore. For a long time my only sensations were caused

AN INDIAN JOURNEY

by the damp twigs which stroked my face. I listened to the boatmen as they called to one another in the darkness. At long intervals there came a whitish or reddish gleam of light. Against such a background I could see huge leaves, or the spears of the tall rushes. Once a great marsh fowl took wing with a penetrating cry which rang across the water for a considerable time.

"Panya," I called.

Now a light was visible on the shore. I could make out a narrow sandbank to which the boat had been moored. Overhead was a leafy alley. So thick was the foliage that the impression produced was that we were in a green cavern, in the midst of which stood Panya, clad in white, holding a torch aloft, and beckoning to me.

The boatmen needed a few hours' rest. A semicircle of fires protected us on the landward side, and soon the men were sleeping soundly on their mats. Panya squatted opposite me beside the fire, carrying on an uninterrupted soliloquy in tones of suppressed excitement. I noted in him the restlessness of the tropical summer night. The sight of the oarsmen at work had roused in me strangely vivid memories of savage deeds. Over the germinating stillness that encompassed us, there brooded a spirit of amorous impulses and a foreboding of sudden and futile death. It seemed as if the fiercely luxuriant vegetation, in the urge of its vital impetus, was, for all its outward tranquillity, lusting for our lives. My blood throbbed in finger tips, temples, and throat.

After a time, Panya came to the end of his discourse.

AN INDIAN JOURNEY

Twisting a torch out of dry lianas and touchwood, he poured oil over it and kindled it at the fire.

"Whither away, Panya?"

"To the women," he answered gruffly.

For a time I watched the red sheen of his torch as he marched through the thicket, whirling the brand above and around him to scare wild beasts, waving it in time with his swift, soft footsteps. I was left alone at the fireside with Elijah. Pasha lay asleep in the boat. He had spread his mat upon the boxes, and was guarding my property even in his slumbers.

V ••••• JUNGLE FOLK ••••• V

HEN the wind was in a favourable quarter, Panya could smell the villages before we reached them.

"We're coming to a village soon, Sahib," he would say. "We'd better pitch our tent."

The reason for camping close to a village was proximity to a place where we could be sure of getting fresh water, rice, and bananas, and sometimes fowls and eggs as well. We had great difficulty in finding porters, for two men or women were generally needed even for a light load. Moreover, the bearers usually grew homesick after two or three days, and deserted, although it was my practice not to pay them until the end of their term of service. They were the less inclined to bother about the wages, because when they left they would as a rule steal something which seemed a full compensation to them although the loss was never very considerable to me.

Every time one of our slaves absconded, Panya expressed the fervent hope that the panther might seize the rascal on his flight. The boy was perfectly sincere and quite unfeeling in the matter, and he never varied as regards the beast of prey to strike down the fugitive. In such emergencies we would often camp for days beside the track or in the midst of the jungle, smoking, sleeping, hunting. I could not discover my place on the map, but this was of no consequence, for I knew the extent of the jungle, and sun and compass gave me my direction. The rivers, too, which we crossed at the fords or in native boats, showed us that in the main we had not lost our bearings. Besides, had I any particular goal?

One of the young porters remained with us for a considerable time, finding favour with me; and at length also with Panya, which was altogether exceptional. Gurumahu by name, he was a lad of about eighteen, tall and very thin, but alert and vigorous. He was a convert to Islam, having based extensive hopes upon the liberties which this doctrine would permit him to enjoy. Unfortunately, his gentle disposition made it impossible for him to avail himself of his opportunities. After conversion, he was just as much afraid of the Brahmins as he had been before, and did not change his mode of life in the least. Our intimacy with him dated from one of the thefts which had now grown familiar, for his insatiable desire for wealth had inspired him with a craving for my copper cooking pots.

By good fortune, Gurumahu was detected in the act, for we should have been greatly embarrassed had he got safely away with his booty. We had Elijah to thank—although Panya claimed the credit. Our tent was pitched on the margin of the open country, so that from the entry there was a view over a rolling plain. I was awakened by the dog's growling, to see Gurumahu in the moonlight running away with a copper saucepan in each hand, running as if the Devil were behind him. I seized my revolver, and fired in the air. The absconder was probably out of range, and of course I had no wish to kill him. These drastic measures are out of place in India, for the Hindus have not such a taste for death as the African negroes (if travellers' tales be true). But I knew that the bang would have a good effect upon the conscience of the plunderer, who himself owned a great fire-arm of which more later. With a yell, Gurumahu threw himself face downwards on the ground, and on either hand the saucepans, gleaming in the moonlight, rolled away through the grass.

Since everything remained quiet and he saw no pursuer, he sat up cautiously, and began to feel his limbs one after another. Attention was first given to the legs, which were doubtless of supreme importance to him in his present situation. Next came the turn of the body and the arms. Finally he made sure that his head, like the rest, was in its place and in working order. Then he leaped to his feet, and ran away with great bounds, without another glance at the copper saucepans which had been denied him.

Panya retrieved them, and though in a temper, cleaned them with the utmost care.

"The panther will make short work of the fellow," said he, and angrily fed the fire with brushwood. His ill-humour arose from the fact that the pistol shot had broken

AN INDIAN JOURNEY

his sleep. Tacitly, and not without concern, I gave up Gurumahu for lost, though not necessarily by Panya's chosen road. I was mistaken, however, for the lad crept back into camp towards noon next day. Probably he had found loneliness in the jungle by night little to his taste; or maybe the smell of the curry which was cooking for dinner had allured him. Panya haled him before me with a solemn air. The poor criminal looked as if he had just been pulled out of the water.

"I am going to kill you," I said quietly.

He sprang high in the air, and then threw himself on the ground before me.

"Shall I hang him?" enquired Panya in a callous tone, which made me realise how mean was my own threat. Remarkable is the readiness with which we can perceive injustice when another commits it.

"He has eaten a whole glassful of salt," reported Panya in a matter-of-fact way. "If he has not stolen a bottle of whiskey, that is only because he could not find it."

"Did you steal because you were hungry? Where have you been hiding all the morning?" I enquired of the evildoer.

He raised his head and tried to meet my eyes—a thing which the natives of out-of-the-way parts can rarely do, when the eyes they have to face are blue, and when they seldom come in contact with Europeans. Gurumahu, however, understood my quizzical expression, and began to laugh as unrestrainedly as a child.

"You are kind to me, Sahib," he began hesitatingly. Then, speaking more confidently, he continued: "You are

AN INDIAN JOURNEY

not haughty and stern like the English. I will watch over your saucepans till I die."

"If that's all you are going to do, you may as well be off to the swamps again," said Panya grumblingly; but Guru would allow nothing to disturb the joy he felt in his newly granted life. As the two went away, I heard him say cheekily to my boy:

"Has a Sahib ever shot at you, infidel? You are not worth powder and shot. That is why you still live to grovel at your master's feet. I have fought with him!"

"True, O eater of copper," rejoined Panya. "It is a mercy that you did not utterly destroy him, tree-louse!"

Henceforward Gurumahu stayed with us. We called him Guru for short. He had quite a string of melodious names in addition to Gurumahu, but the latter was the one he preferred.

On one occasion we were benighted, despite Panya's caution. The darkness surprised us on the marshy bank of a river. Guru sniffed the damp night air as he peered across the water towards the palm grove upon the opposite bank, where after a time we could see a faint light flickering. When the tent had been pitched and the fires kindled, we heard the plash of oars in the river. The noise reverberated over the tent; there was a rustling among the trees; then all was still.

"The mangroves have eyes now," said Panya. "These must be feather-brained folk, for they have no fear of the panther."

In this predicament we could put no trust in Elijah, for his temperament made it impossible for him to give night-

AN INDIAN JOURNEY

prowlers a harmless fright by barking at them. When we heard a panther coughing near the camp, it was Elijah's custom to withdraw into the innermost recesses of the tent; not, of course, because he was afraid, but merely because he thought he would be more comfortable there.

That day I had shot a jay-thrush. I was plucking the brown feathers; and the handsome head, marked with light-blue rings round the eyes, was hanging across my knee. But for the lack of these pale rings round them, Guru's eyes as he watched me were as fixed and lifeless as those of the dead bird. He could not understand how I could bring myself to eat a creature which has probably been animated by a transmigrated soul. Panya had long since been emancipated from all such relics of his tribal philosophy. The water was boiling in the copper saucepan, and a multitude of nocturnal insects had collected in the firelight, fluttering round the flames like coloured sparks, or glaring from the leaves at this incomprehensible red life whose ardours lured them to death.

Panya now thoughtfully brought me the remnants of my razor, which resembled a pocket saw, and was occasionally used as such. A cook of mine had once slaughtered a goat with it; for we Europeans must sometimes pay the penalty when we initiate an unsophisticated race into our barbarous customs. A shadow of this barbarism had for a long time been fitfully haunting my chin and cheeks, rivalling the undergrowth of the jungle in its scrubby growth. Guru had rifled some nests in the jungle, and brought me the eggs. We boiled a few of them—those that were not just on the point of hatching. Panya chewed betel as he watched me. He had a fine instinct for the occasions when I was glad to do some work, and for those when he had to relieve me. Of late, too, he had felt exalted by his rôle of cicerone, and he set about his tasks with a new sense of splendid freedom. Pasha was cleaning palm buds, which of all the vegetables eaten in India have the most agreeable and delicate flavour. They are now a forbidden article of diet, for the removal of the bud is fatal to the life of the tree. The whitish growing-point of the cabbage palm is cut away. It has a taste and a smell resembling those of fresh hazel nuts. Prepared with oil and fruit-juice, it makes a better salad than any known to European cooks.

"Shall I ask the people whether they have mango trees in their village?" said Guru suddenly.

"What people?" I asked in astonishment.

"Those," answered Guru, pointing.

Thereupon I perceived brown faces peering from among the mangrove-trees, showing up in the firelight. I had long become used to never being alone, and yet I was continually being startled afresh. Counting the faces, I made out five at first, then ten, and finally about twenty, large and small. It seemed that the whole village had assembled.

I sent Guru over to them. The faces vanished. In the darkness there ensued a lively and ever livelier parley. At length torches were lighted, and the oarsmen clattered into their dug-out. I should have been glad to have a talk with them, but they were too timid. However, they brought us everything we wanted. The inhabitants of this part of the country, like those of the Eastern Ghats,

AN INDIAN JOURNEY

are primitive indigens, and have mixed hardly at all with the Aryan immigrants. Their skin is almost black, and their features are more like those of negroes than those of Hindus. They are at a very low level of civilisation, but are harmless and pacifically inclined. Their religion has remained at the infantile stage of paganism. They pray to wooden idols, and only here and there has a glimmer of light from the Brahministic or Buddhistic doctrine penetrated their intellectual world. In their pantheon we occasionally find a corrupt form of one of the many incarnations of Brahman, but they have no living idea of the meaning of this divinity.

In favourable seasons their wants are easily supplied. They bring pepper to the little Malabar ports, where the native dealers pay them a very moderate price. Their diet consists mainly of fruits and nuts. Some eat fish. It is said that a few eat meat, but I never saw anything of the kind. The earth in front of their palm-leaf huts is stamped flat, and here they spread out the peppercorns to dry in the sun. The berries are carefully arranged in squares, each square being of a different tint according to the stage of the drying process, so that the colours range from juicy green to profound black. The chief worldly wealth of these indigens consists of children. Never have I seen so many little children as in their villages. With pot bellies and running noses, the youngsters stood in black rows like organ pipes in front of the huts, all agape as we came by.

I shall never forget the evening and the night of which I have been speaking, for under my very eyes a vital spark was extinguished in the jungle. I had no idea what was the hour, when a loud cry awakened me. Panya jumped to his feet. Half-awakened, he staggered against my hammock; I was nearly thrown to the ground, and for a moment mistook him for an enemy. The fire was almost out. Panya hastened to the glowing embers and in a trice had blown them to a flame. The lamentable cry was repeated. In the thick darkness, nothing was visible beyond the tree stems close to the fire and reflecting its light. They gleamed with a fantastic air of unreality, resembling limbless monsters with shapeless heads formed by the foliage, crowding into a narrow red-lighted room. Pasha was beside the second fire, which Guru was busily fanning, and called out something.

"What did he say?" I asked Panya.

"A woman is crying out in terror of death," answered Panya, who had not yet grasped what was amiss.

Coming forth from the tent, I could now see torches moving in the forest, and could discern the dusky forms of the savages. My heart was racked by a woman's wail. Rarely have I heard so piteous an expression of grief and despair. It was an animal cry of pain, and yet voiced the misery of the human spirit. I felt as if a ghost were walking in the night, and I had repeatedly to pull myself together to keep my energies from being paralysed and to avoid succumbing to a sense of horror.

"Make a light," I shouted.

A cloud of yellow smoke enveloped us, and then a tall red column flickered in its midst. Guru cried:

"It is the mother!"

A cluster of naked figures appeared, timid and yet eager,

AN INDIAN JOURNEY

carrying a recumbent form upon a stretcher improvised out of branches. A woman with black locks streaming across her face, gesticulating wildly, called to me something unintelligible. Despite her intense excitement, despite the urgency of her errand, she did not venture close to me, but I could now make out that her expression was one of mingled dread and hope.

On the stretcher lay a girl of twelve or thirteen, scantily covered with a parti-coloured strip of cotton. Beneath this her slender form was contorted. I heard a dull moaning, a strangled gurgling.

Guru groaned compassionately, and shivered.

"The cobra," said Panya. "The mother has come to you for help."

My heart bled under the glances of the old woman, a touching and pitiable figure as she stood before me in her pain and hideousness. Her breasts were pendulous and flaccid; her withered face was convulsed. Her lamentations had ceased, for now she was dumb with expectation; craning forwards she peered into my face, seeming to believe that at my pleasure I could give death or life to her daughter.

With the other villagers, the girl had been prowling round our camp to catch sight of the strange man from a foreign world, from a world which lay beyond the sea and was full of mysteries and wonders. In her eagerness for the novel and the incomprehensible, she had forgotten the caution which is indispensable in the jungle, the caution which had been impressed on her from earliest childhood. Amid the gloom, she had felt the little prick which at the

AN INDIAN JOURNEY

outset her heart would not believe to be the terrible doom; she had stifled her fears notwithstanding the sudden anguish of collapse and the feeling as if dark wings were brushing her temples. It must have been a thorn. Then had come giddiness, swimming in the head, failing pulse. The hands were cramped, and by degrees all the limbs, as if there were glass splinters in the blood, tearing the vessels. At length the dread certainty found vent in a cry:

"The Queen of Darkness!"

The jungle was filled with this cry, at once a cry of veneration for the deity and a cry of horror and lamentation.

It was too late. I lanced the wound, which was no more than a needle prick on the foot, a prick with blackened margins; but from the knife-cut the blood came sluggishly, no longer red and warm. We plied the child with whiskey, but for all our endeavours we could not get her to swallow the fierce spirit. Her eyes seemed to reproach those whose cruel aid took the form of new inflictions. The cautery is only of use in the first instant after the bite, and in any case I could never have brought myself to add a fresh torment to those from which the little frame was already suffering. Let the child die in peace, exclaimed a voice within me. It is her last privilege on earth.

My heart was wrung by the mother's eyes. In this supreme hour I had no help to give her beyond sympathy. She sank upon the ground with a prolonged wail, and lay mute for the rest of the night, a dark bundle of clothing against the white wall of the hut.

AN INDIAN JOURNEY

When the child was dead, there was borne in on me with a crude intensity the bitter realisation of human impotence. We fail so utterly to be what at our best we fain would be. Where is the power which we glimpse in our craving for fulfilment; where the nobility which our good feeling makes us seek; where the faith that moves mountains?

At once tenderly sad, charming, and ardent, were these days, the most memorable of my life. Often we remained encamped for a considerable time in one spot, my goal and the passage of time forgotten. The green eyes of the jungle and the silvery breath of the night air in the open country put a spell upon me; thought gave place to reverie; day was an indefeasible certitude of the joy of life, and night a formless dream. The vigorous, tranquil, and patient growth of the plants which claimed every corner of the earth, gradually robbed my mind of the consciousness of its own rights. Cradled in wonder and animated by the will of another existence than my own, I moved onwards as if walking in sleep; and yet at the same time vigilant, and profoundly permeated with a glowing faith in the sacredness of being. The marshy poison of the forest held sway over me—the forest whose queen and goddess had appeared to me in all her dread majesty; I saw the spirit of fever lurking in the damp, twilit arcades; my power of active resistance had declined to no more than vague hope in good luck. This teeming and fermenting fertility of the marsh would take my body likewise into itself, and would make it blossom as new life, were it to

AN INDIAN JOURNEY

grasp that body in its tentacles. The forest was mightier than man.

One night I was lying in the tent upon a couch of leaves, for I had wearied of the unstable flexibility of the hammock. Guru had fallen asleep over the fire. He was squatting in front of the triangular entry to the tent. His head was sunk between his knees, so that he looked as if he had been decapitated; and his ancient Arab flint-lock, a weapon of enormous length, towered over him like a flagstaff. He was passionately fond of this fire-arm, and generally took it with him wherever he went, especially when there was any likelihood of encountering human beings. At the same time he had a firm conviction that the flint-lock would never play him the trick of going off. His expectations were not likely to be disappointed, for it was at least a hundred years old, must have travelled all over the East from Soudan to Singapore, and was incapable of being loaded or discharged. But Guru was sleeping in the primeval forest, sure that his weapon would protect him; for he had absolute confidence in the virtues of this long talisman.

That day we had been marching through the foothills, where the jungle, now growing thinner, thrusts fingers upwards into the mountain valleys. A clear stream was flowing down the rocky bed. Since the ground was too uneven and overgrown for farther upward progress, we had turned back along the bank of the stream, to reach a hamlet consisting of about ten palm-leaf huts, Itupah by name. We had pitched our tent close to this settlement, and had lighted the camp fire. The natives came to offer us fruits,

AN INDIAN JOURNEY

but did not stay long, for to their minds our whole equipment smacked of magic and danger.

I could not sleep. The calls of the wild beasts and the light of the moon made me restless. Panya had slipped away to the hamlet, in search of love adventures. My arrival at Itupah had aroused considerable excitement, and Panya was determined to provide a justification for it. The patches of moonlight at the tent door looked like cuttings of white paper. The air was full of the noise of the cicadas; the sound was like that of fine silver wire being filed with frenzied haste by mad prisoners.

There came a rustle from the corner of the tent, and glancing in that direction I caught sight of a little beast which at first I took for a marten. It sat perfectly still now that my movement had aroused its fears, contemplating me with huge black eyes, protuberant and close set like those of a monkey. The slender head was not much larger than a walnut in the husk. The fur was greyish-brown like that of a squirrel in winter.

I was much taken with this little beast, so I made advances.

"Come nearer," I said, and gently whistled a couple of notes, repeating them again and again. The animal did not stir, and I looked round for some means of allurement. When I moved my hand towards a biscuit which was on the ground near me, there was a noiseless leap in the corner, and the space was void. After a time, however, a shadow glided across the patch of moonlight, and the little stranger was there once more, manifestly a prey to curiosity. The black eyes were widely opened with astonishment; they seemed to be sucking me in as a new phenomenon; never have I been so stared at. The creature seemed intensely eager to discover its own kinship to me, to learn what had brought me from my distant home to the neighbourhood of Itupah and to the vicinity of its own dwelling. I did not know, but I would not have given a false explanation.

"Have you any family?" I asked gently.

The animal vanished. At this early stage of our acquaintance the question may have been a trifle impertinent. After a time, however, the beast reappeared at the very same spot, between our store of salt and Panya's sandals. It seemed to have noticed by this time that my incantations were not so dangerous as it had thought at first, so it came a little nearer to stare the better.

I was sorry that I had nothing suitable to offer my guest, and that my attempts at hospitality aroused its suspicions.

"You seem to be a night walker," I began cautiously. "Your eyes show it, and the fact that we meet at such an hour. Please don't draw any false inferences from the miscellany of articles you are now looking at. We are long creatures; we walk about on our hind legs; but essentially we are stirred by the same motives as you. They can be summed up in a few words: happiness, sunshine, love, and sleep. Over these desires, something else watches, an unceasing hope that in days to come things will be much better than they are now. Like desires are expressed by your great eyes. Is the impulse which has brought you into my tent fundamentally different from those which have led me into the wilderness which is your home?"

I was answered by a clear, angry hiss, which chilled me to the marrow; and, as instant accompaniment, there was a rustling in the leaves of my couch. It behoved me to lie still, unless my jungle pilgrimage were to be brought to an untimely end. . . .

I now knew who my first visitor was, but I was far more concerned by the knowledge of what was close to me among the withered leaves. The little quadruped began to rock gently to and fro, uttering the while at intervals a sharp cry, betwixt a hiss and a growl, which was directed towards my bedfellow. Now from the couch of leaves a form emerged, making swiftly for the exit, like the flow of a thick, dark fluid. A little shadow from the corner of the tent glided after the snake with the speed of lightning, and then from without came a turmoil of rustling and thrashing sounds, interspersed with spitting, hissing, and snorting. Then silence, and I could hear nothing but the troubled beating of my own heart as I watched the patches of moonlight, until gradually the monotonous song of the cicadas dominated the night once more. To my fancy they had been silent while the destiny of other creatures of the night had been fought out under my eyes.

How strangely different the fulfilment of our wishes often is from our anticipations! I had frequently heard of this marvellous animal, which is reckoned in India to be the most formidable enemy of the snake, and which the English often keep as a pet and for protection against cobras; but I had pictured my meeting with the mongoose

AN INDIAN JOURNEY

in a very different fashion. What had I seen and heard beyond a crouch and a spring, punctuated by a few cries of battle, fear, and lust of life? Shadowy, almost unreal, the beast had looked, greyish in the half light, devoid of that emotional halo which foreknowledge would have given to the incident. It is memory which creates the figure of the hero. Was this all? How will it fare with the fleeting little life which we allow to slip away in anticipations?

Often when I set out from the tent through the jungle, gun on shoulder, and Elijah at heel, from the margin of the river I saw the crocodiles basking on the sandbanks. They lay anyhow, sometimes even across one another—which seemed to me very uncomfortable. As a rule the expression of their long faces was one of extreme complacency. Their little eyes sparkled merrily; and their great mouths, often wide open, seemed to be smiling. Their demeanour indicated how pleasant they found the sun to their hard, scaly skin; it was difficult to think any harm of them. Sometimes there came a gurgle from their soft, yellow throats.

I never saw any that were more than six or seven feet long. Their African congeners must belong to another species, and are far more formidable in appearance. Sometimes I fired at one of these huge lizards. Of course I may have missed, but if I did hit any of them they were always able to make for the water. The report usually cleared the sandbank. These creatures bid farewell with a speed that savours of rudeness. They shoot into the water like torpedoes, without any apparent movement of

AN INDIAN JOURNEY

the legs. To the onlooker it appears as if they had been attached to the river by a stretched piece of elastic and had suddenly been let go. They are splendid swimmers, and when swimming they look like pike; but they are extraordinarily timid, and are dangerous only to the smaller quadrupeds which come down to the stream to drink. One morning I threw them the remnants of an antelope. I had myself been able to enjoy no more than a cut from the saddle, for the rest had been spoiled by the sun or the jackals. I was horrified at the insensate greed of this mob of river dwellers. Within a couple of minutes, the body had been torn to rags, and had vanished in a pool of bloody foam. At noon the monsters were again basking in the sun and smiling, while the broad and turbid stream rippled on its course, reflecting the fierce midday sun in shafts of light that were acutely painful to eyes accustomed to the twilight of the jungle.

One day I was sitting near the tent among the interlacing aërial roots of a banyan tree, enjoying the early sunshine and cleaning my fowling-piece, when there came a rustle from the mangroves close at hand. When I turned, I saw a little native boy, dumb with fear. His eyes were expressionless, like two round, black mirrors, and his mouth was wide open. It was natural he should be startled, for I had been bathing, and was wearing what without exaggeration may be described as nothing at all. The youngster had never expected, on his way to the river, to encounter this white apparition.

He trembled violently, and swallowed, but did not venture to move his limbs. This was worse than a tiger; it

AN INDIAN JOURNEY

was a terrible wood demon! The strange being held an incomprehensible shining object across its knees. It glistened; it had eyes which one could not face without risking destruction. But when this streaming monster now suddenly sneezed, from the terror-stricken little breast there came a yell of alarm, and the lad obviously thought all was up with him. He threw himself on the ground, buried his face in the herbage, and continued to utter a monotonous wail, in which he was probably commending himself to the favour of one of his idols.

I did not know what to do to calm the poor little wretch. If I had touched him, he would have died of fright, so I let him lie where he was for a time, while I noted that his toilet was in the same primitive stage as my own. Then it occurred to me that I would whistle to him in a simple and sentimental manner. This, I thought, could not fail to reassure him. I began with an ancient lullaby, passed from that to a hymn, and finished up with "God save the King."

It worked. Without raising his head, my friend twisted his dusky face so that with one eye he could see about as far as my knees. Of course he was still positive that I must be an ogre, but apparently I was not hungry that morning. I quietly gave him to understand that he was to get up. He obeyed, still trembling, but obviously astonished that I could speak like a reasonable being, and could actually use his own tongue. He was still all eyes, and these eyes expressed a single wish, to be granted leave to depart. He could peer at me far more comfortably out

AN INDIAN JOURNEY

of a hiding-place, and why should he run the risk of being so close to me?

But his views changed when I felt in the pockets of my clothes and held out an anna towards him. Of course he saw the coin immediately, but not for some time did the idea that he was to take it dawn in his brain. The very notion seemed impossible. Well did he know the value of these round discs of metal. His father sometimes brought them back from the seaport, after a visit there with pepper and ginger. The owner of such a coin could command anything—all the glories of the world—coloured cloth, sweets, rice, and cassava bread. He would have power over all the boys of the district.

When he at length realised that my only present design was to make this sacrifice, he departed, uneaten, with his treasure. Very likely he will remember me a few years hence, when he has become a young man, and has earned for himself plenty of annas in the seaports. By then his opinions concerning white men will have changed, in more senses than one.

As the days passed, I began more and more to feel that something was wrong with me. Casting about for the cause, I blamed now one thing, now another. One day I felt sure that the drinking water was at fault; next I would fancy I was smoking too much, or that some unfamiliar fruit had disagreed with me; then I would suppose that my uneasy symptoms were due to insomnia, or were the effect of the damp, over-heated aromatic air. Panya often looked at me askance, without realising that I was aware of his glances, and that they annoyed me. I was unjust and harsh to him, but he was patient and was no longer sulky. He had of late changed a good deal. He seemed to have a new sense of responsibility, as if he were training himself in strength and virtue. I was making him a poor return for this transformation, but I could not help myself.

I sometimes felt as if my brain had grown very small, and as if it were tossing and gyrating within the cranium like one of those balls that one sees moving about in a closed vessel of water. I tried all kinds of remedies except the only one which could have helped me—flight from the swampy jungle.

In the morning I longed for noon, when the insects would buzz about happily; when the huge butterflies, with their incredibly vivid tints of blue or green would flit silently from blossom to blossom; when the whole world would luxuriate in the heat. In the discomfort of the early afternoon hours I looked forward to the evening and in the evening to the night with its cries of love and of hunting and with its stars sparkling in the black abysses of the sky. Night and day no longer signified to me sleep and waking; they were merely changing lineaments of the visage of India, magically interwoven, mystically transformed.

My home had vanished from memory. Europe had become a noisy and unpleasant dream, full of needless bustle. I smiled compassionately when I recalled the fuss that I had made over the petty happenings of my restless past. The activities of great cities seemed to me nothing more than the clamorous and gaudy expressions of a false view of life. Now sleeping and waking succeeded one another like fleeting seasons. The passage of day into night and of night into day, aroused no more than a vague sense of change. The innocent simplicity of the vegetation which enveloped me as with a living vesture, was the strongest influence that affected my slowly ebbing intellectual energies.

At times the desire to escape from this garment of vegetation drove me out of the darkness of the jungle to the margin of the open country. I longed to see the sky and the far-flung brown hills. Thus emerging from the woodland, I felt as if liberated from trammels by a silent storm of light. Often we would break camp in the middle of the night, retrace our steps along the road we had laboriously traversed the day before, to pitch the tent once more beside the ashes of the abandoned fires. I felt as if the plants held me from drawing breath, as if they robbed me of what was essential to my own life to satisfy their vital needs. Often I detected myself casting malicious glances at some flowering shrub whose display of love passion in purple blossoms filled me with rage and hatred, and at the same time inspired me with a sense of self-sacrificing humility.

By degrees my manuscripts and books had fallen victims to the flames of our camp fires. With spiteful gratification I watched the white leaves shrivel up in the glow, and I enjoyed a sense of relief when the charred pages crumbled into dust. There was one only of my books, a trivial little volume, which I preserved for a long time. I am sure that the sole thing which saved it from destruction was that the binding was ornamented with an intricate design in gold. This decoration was unpleasing, meaningless, and obtrusive; but it gave me pleasure to follow the lines with my weary eyes. Once I tried to remember where letters would be awaiting me. I thought of Bombay, Goa, and Madras; but could not decide.

With a ringing in my ears, produced by quinine, a noise resembling that heard when a great sea-shell is held close to the ear, during the silent hours of the noonday heat, lying with closed eyes, I would often dream of winter. Again and again the same vision recurred. I was looking at a grey valley in the evening mist. As the light failed, the snow on the rocks assumed a bluish tint. An icy wind ruffled the dark waters of the river, down which blocks of ice were floating. These boomed against one another with a loud noise. On some of the drifting floes, ravens perched. Of a sudden, the deadly chill took the form of lancinating pains in forehead and cheeks; my chest swelled as if bursting with the cold. Sometimes I would fall asleep while shivering amid such visions, to be tormented with wild dreams, so that sleep brought no refreshment.

One night I dreamed that I had fallen asleep in a mountain gorge close to the ocean. I was awakened by the voices of two men, their tones having a strange kinship with the murmur of the waters. Half rising, I rested my elbows on the sand, and looked in amazement. The sun had sunk beneath the sea, and was shining out of the depths through the water. Although it looked like a red-hot ball, the light in the air was pale and greenish, inter-

AN INDIAN JOURNEY

spersed with strange waves of shadow, probably caused by the waves of the sea.

The two men were standing close together on the sand, which shone like turquoise. Their arms were hanging loosely by their sides, and from beneath their brows there looked at me quiet eyes of a uniform light-blue colour. I could not see any distinction of pupil. Their skins were amber-coloured; their hair was almost white; they were broad shouldered but lean, and their hips were so slender that their sides seemed to run obliquely in straight lines from the armpits to the ankles. Their temples were bound about with a scarf of eosin-red, which opened out like a fan over the left shoulder, to disappear behind it.

This was all the clothing worn by the two, as they stood quietly before me in the greenish light with its mysterious waves of shadow. It seemed to me as if they were smiling, inquisitively rather than mockingly. At length they began a conversation, endeavouring to produce the impression that they completely ignored my scrutiny, though I realised that they were talking at me. They smiled furtively and disagreeably, casting stealthy glances towards me from time to time. Then one of them pointed at the rocks in a ravine where, halfway up the hills, a deep horizontal groove was visible.

"Yes," rejoined the other, "that is the old sea line, the last one. But what has become of the sea line of our fathers?"

"The hilltops are sinking too rapidly," said the first. "The new world will be small."

Much which they went on to say or hint was beyond my

AN INDIAN JOURNEY

comprehension, but I realised that they were speaking of lost realms whose civilisation had vanished ages ago beneath the sea sand, and they murmured of the imminence of a day when the present distribution of earth and water was to be changed. Overwhelmed with consternation, I had a vision of these realms now hidden in the sea, and I saw them, after their resurrection, gradually emerging from their sandy investment under the influence of sun, wind, and rain. I did not dare to question the men, although I was burning with eagerness to profit by their experiences. It seemed as if they could read in my face a desire to rob them of their secrets, for they touched one another on the shoulder, turned seaward, and vanished into the depths of the waters, as if they were moving through the air. I caught sight of them once more for a moment, as they passed over the sun, which had now sunk very low. Then I fell asleep, in a mood of sadness more intense than I had ever known, a mood such as can be experienced only in slumber.

Another time in a dream some one gave me a warship with a crew of women, so that I could attack my enemies. Unfortunately, however, these enemies, three in number, were land dwellers. I therefore dismissed the crew of ladies, to the delight of my three opponents. I discharged the guns of my ship at the gulls, but they pecked at the cannon balls, waiting for this purpose at the very mouths of the cannon—it was really most annoying. I perceived that I should do no good that way, but meanwhile I was light-heartedly solving a number of problems by which I had hitherto been incredibly perplexed. In the end it

AN INDIAN JOURNEY

occurred to me that for such intellectual experiments it was necessary to crawl about underground, which I did persistently, and with huge delight.

After many dreams of this sort, most of which I have forgotten, I came to my senses one noontide, shivering in the midday heat, and lying in a corner of the tent with a dry mouth and a horrible sense of vacancy in the forehead. Surrendering myself passively to Panya's ministrations, I allowed him to roll me up in rugs, and awaited death in the flames of these fantastic fires of my blood and my imagination, flames fanned by evil demons.

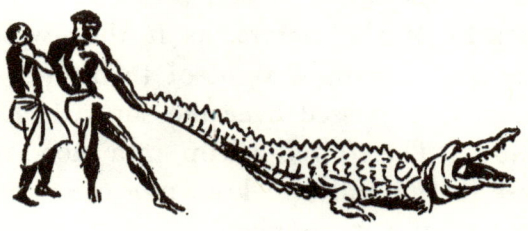

VI .... FEVER VI

IN a vague hour which was neither in the morning nor in the evening, I awoke with a definite realisation that I had died on the morning after the memorable night with Huc the monkey. After death there must ensue a strange half-slumber of the dying senses, wherein we are still deluded with a semblance of the continuance of life, a sort of persistent memory of the body, which will not yet admit its doom. The soul has fled, but bodily existence is sustained for a time in a pitiful counterfeit by the hopes of our heart. All the experiences I had undergone from that morning down to the present time must have been traversed in this phase. I smiled with mournful contempt as I moved to and fro through the softly tinkling spheres which formed my present habitation. I was glad, however, that consciousness still persisted; and I was well content to have realised at length that I was dead. I now plainly perceived the tormenting uncertainty surrounding all that had happened to me of late. Had not these impressions emerged, as it were, out of grey mirrors, to disappear into others of the same kind, in weird gyrations, and with a lamentable remoteness from reality? In this new revelation as to my death, which in my faint-hearted clinging to life I had hitherto refused to admit, I determined with marvellous composure that in future I would render service to memory alone. At the same time I was strangely disturbed by Panya's face, which appeared to me from time to time, looking hazy and huge like a shadowy cloud, interfering with my progress through the shimmering universe, and haunting me with a tiresome persistency. I was under no delusions. It was clear to me that the thirst with which my body raged was the thirst of my soul for knowledge. I felt myself lucky that this was the only way in which I suffered.

Some one spoke to me. Deliberately, for a considerable time I paid no heed, for I was firmly convinced that no one had any right to address a dead man. Could not this futile creature realise that the dead have something better to do than to concern themselves with the perishable gawds which are the chief interest of those who live on earth—a poor little place that cannot even keep still, but must dance for ever in ludicrous dependence round the sun? At length I decided that I would make sure of being left in peace, and, with that admirable freedom of spirit which only the dead know, I issued an order for silence. But then I perceived that my own ego was sitting beside me smoking. He had annexed my pipe, my clothes, and my shoes, and was wearing my snake-ring with its five golden coils, a snake with sapphire eyes and a crown of diamonds. I found it difficult to assume the right manner, for this is not easy to achieve towards a person whom one has often tricked during life. My ego smiled at me encouragingly, but I would not allow myself to be humbugged. I knew that smile, for we know the smile which we use to deceive others, we know what our own smile hides. For some reason or other I said quickly and angrily:

"Whatever you do, please don't philosophise!"

My ego answered genially, that he had no thought of doing anything of the kind, and that in view of my severance from life (a severance which I had at length realised), I no longer had any concern with the problems of being and not-being.

It was a fascinating experience to hear my own voice from the lips of my double; but something in the tones showed a calm self-possession far excelling the embarrassment I had often manifested when using this same voice. I was seriously annoyed, for I realised in what respects I had fallen short when I was alive.

"Do you see what hidden merits I used to possess?" I enquired. However, my annoyance speedily vanished, for there was really something most impressive about this clarified ego with whom I was now confronted.

"Did I ever make such an impression upon one of my fellows as you are now making upon me?" I enquired ceremoniously.

"Don't be so stiff in your manner. You were quite friendly a moment ago," said my ego cordially, and without offensive patronage. "It's time we came to an understanding."

I was of the same mind. "You may as well give me my ring, then," I said.

AN INDIAN JOURNEY

Thereupon the double, as if myself had been sitting there, drew the ring from his finger with precisely the same gestures I had been wont to use when anyone asked me to show him the ring. I tried to slip it on, but my finger broke in two.

"Damn it all, am I as far gone as that, Sahib?" I testily enquired.

My ego took the finger and carefully put it away in his pocket, the very pocket that I always kept ready for any unconsidered trifles.

"Are we still in India?" I asked, but the instant I had spoken I became aware that the circumstance was no longer of any moment to me. "What on earth are you doing here?" was my next question, which was perhaps a trifle rude; for my ego, since he was the double of myself, was not likely to have come without some definite purpose.

In fact the double now rose to his feet, settled his coat, shook his legs to straighten his trousers, and smoothed his hair. I knew, of course, what this meant. I was to be shown my grave.

"You must not expect too much," came from the double. "Panya has buried you in the forest, barely an ell deep, and the forest flowers are growing across your eyes."

These were the last words I heard. I could see no one now, and I became aware that I was lying in my grave. For a moment, thoughts continued to flow through my mind, and then I was overpowered by an indescribable feeling of repose.

No words can picture it. Never have I had any pleasant experience comparable to this repose. Once when I was

AN INDIAN JOURNEY

alive, after a long and fatiguing journey, full of unwholesome haste and tormenting anticipations, I reached my goal. Here came the consolation of certainty, and I found myself lying on a cool, white bed, in a quiet room whose window commanded a view of the mountains. The few minutes in which, before falling asleep, I enjoyed the sense of rest stealing over my tired body, are perhaps remotely comparable to my happy condition now that I lay in my grave. You must, however, imagine the sense of well-being increased up to the verge of unconsciousness, a feeling akin to that of the peaceful ecstasy which might be induced by listening to celestial music.

My hands were crossed upon my breast; I was lying stretched on my back: the heavy covering of earth was a pleasant burden—the loving hands of a mother could not have rested more gently upon my face. I was aware of an equable, strong pulsation, the origin of which was hidden from me, but which filled me with content. As long as one at least of the living creatures in the world continued to think lovingly of me, my consciousness remained awake, but was unruffled by painful memories. Indescribably serene and free was the smiling mood with which I recalled earthly happenings, without remembering them in detail. Thus does the grain slumber in the earth during the winter; through its sleep, pass thoughts like a dream of spring, thoughts of the zephyrs, and of the sunshine in which it ripened. The light, the rain, the waving in the breeze, and the reaper, form a gently thrilling reminiscence of the past, disturbed by no sense of sadness, and by no feeling of forlornness. For through this dark realm of slumber there vibrates a strong and regular pulse-beat. The sleeper has no concern whether it is caused by the light-waves of the sun, by the succession of day and night, or by the changing millenniums, for now death is swallowed up in victory. We need only make acquaintance with death in order to learn how futile are the powers which to those who are still entangled in the life of earth seem so invincible a dominion. Now a thousand years are but as yesterday when it is past, and as a watch in the night. No longer did I desire to see any of those whom I had loved, nor was I concerned as to their fate. The pure in heart, who have seen God, cannot be more blessed.

After the lapse of an indefinite time in which I was aware of no change, it seemed to me as if by degrees there was a darkness gathering around me and within me. I was not troubled by any fears that now I was being forgotten, for I was indifferent even to this possibility. Perhaps the fallen leaves were lying more thickly over my resting-place; maybe the earth was no longer circling round the sun, but had come within the orbit of another and greater star, upon which temporal changes took place in accordance with new laws. More and more I lost the consciousness of self, but was not perturbed thereby. Meseemed that such consciousness as was left to me was now concentrated in a single spark, which glowed as hope glows in the hearts of living men.

Gradually I became aware, in a twilit and limitless interval, that a faint light was shining above me, growing quietly, and slowly drawing near. It was a whitish light of low intensity, looking like a pale pencil of rays of delicate contour and slow vitality. It settled down in the region of my heart, not sending forth any illumination through the environing earth, but glowing with gentle serenity. It brought with it the witchery of a distant reminiscence of the sun, and this inspired me with confidence. Then I realised that it was the root of a plant feeling out towards my breast. I was seized with a profound sense of awe, which was neither joy nor hope but which can perhaps be compared with the emotional state which mortals feel when, under some great stress, they burst into tears, without being fully conscious of either pleasure or pain. The nearer the pale, sucking mouth, piously obedient to the laws of its growth, drew to my breast like a winsome child, the more was my fading human consciousness transformed into a blessed sense of universality, sublime in its tranquillity and in its glad readiness to be merged in an invincible realm. Ere long the root of the plant made its way into my heart; and, to the accompaniment of a melodious sound, amid a radiance dazzling in its fresh and happy wildness, my being was drawn forth and upwards into the warm and lightsome hum of the earth's surface.

Above my grave a huge blossom was bursting open, expanding its petals towards the glorious sun.

Now I heard some one approaching with soft footsteps through the dense foliage of the primeval forest, walking along one of the tortuous jungle-paths which are only two or three feet wide and are so overarched with vegetation that they look like green tunnels. The newcomer was a girl, little more than a child, treading gently,

AN INDIAN JOURNEY

but with the proud and erect carriage which is peculiar to mankind among all living creatures. Halting in the twilit shadows where my grave had been dug beneath a tree, and where the newly blossoming flower was now slowly turning as it followed the sun, the girl leaned forwards. In her hair she wore pale-red lotus flowers, and her slender hips were enveloped in a narrow girdle of ochre-coloured silk. A fragrant odour of sandalwood accompanied her like invisible wings of youth.

Round her neck was a double string of red Angola-peas. On one ankle was welded a broad band of gold, which sparkled amid the dewdrops of the undergrowth.

When her eyes, full of an ancient sadness, lighted on the bright-blue, freshly opened flower, it seemed like an encounter between a heavenly radiance and an earthly reflection. The girl did not pluck the flower. She appeared to recall a pleasurable duty, for her face became animated with an expectation tinged with bashfulness. A streamlet flowed among the roots of the trees and over the withered leaves; its limpid waters moved swiftly and silently through the patches of sunshine and shadow. Taking off her necklace, she carefully hung it on one of the betel pepper-vines connecting the branches of the tree with the ground. She laid aside her girdle. Her eyes lighted up with joy in the warm sunshine. But the flowers which decked her luxuriant, swarthy tresses were left in their place, destined to fade there, offered up on the altar of her youthful beauty.

The water grew eloquent at the joyous contact with her sweetness. With a merry smile it rippled over the light-

AN INDIAN JOURNEY

bronze body, which rapturously yielded itself to the caresses of nature, praising its creator with a devotion beyond compare—the creator of the huge forest in which this body was now sheltered, of the countless plants, of all the animals which were breathing in the scented shade, and of the great sun which unceasingly diffused golden happiness for the well-being of its children upon the patient earth.

The girl lay down upon a sunny hillock carpeted with moss, that she might dry herself in the warm air. With charming unconcern she surrendered herself to the light from which no secrets of body or soul are hid, and for which body and soul alike yearn. She seemed to melt into the ground; the pulse-beat of the earth was in unison with the pulse-beat of her blood, and the flowers in her hair exhaled their fragrance in conjunction with the soft aroma of lassitude which rose from her body like a song. The rays of the sun sported over the graceful swell of her little breasts and over her warm, rounded limbs, brightly illuminating here, plunging into mysterious shadow there, mightier than the mightiest conqueror that ever made the world his own, and with the comeliness of a lover who, when troubles are over, brings delight to his beloved. The green forest, rapt in ecstasy, continued to watch this resting triumph of creation, until suddenly, with a clear, piping note, a bird began to sing from amid the foliage. The song expressed a transport of happiness almost painful in its intensity, and from near at hand echoed a jubilant response. The girl thereupon rose to her feet, meditatively donned her girdle and her necklace, and bent once more

AN INDIAN JOURNEY

over the flower in which my being had now become incorporated. Breaking off the blossom, her great eyes smiling as they dwelt on the trembling calyx, she tucked it into her girdle.

What was the reminiscence? Ah, now I could recall it; the great blue flower was the link in my memory. Long since, I had made the acquaintance of this girl and her flower. It was in one of those squandered nights in Bombay, one of those nights which are restless and aimless in their beginnings, and are apt to be all too dismal at the close, nights given up to futilities, in which our high expectations, upborne upon the fumes of wine, perish in the grey hours of morning. But somewhere in our soul, and somewhen in our lifetime, hopes find fulfilment in a splendour akin to the smiling hour of their birth. Hopes are comparable to the buds of slumbering rights, in the twilight of anticipation.

One evening I had wandered forth from the hotel in which for some days I had been waiting for the steamer that was to take me to Singapore. I strolled down the broad and busy street, unprovided for a night of adventure, and with no other aim than the idle one of enjoying the cool evening air for a few minutes as I watched the motley life of the town. But the air was still sultry; it reeked of horses and oil; one could neither breathe freely nor think rationally. Such an atmosphere often seems to be a herald of fever; it confuses our senses and incites us to manifold follies; it teems with the sorrows of loneliness and is overburdened with melancholy; petty devils crav-

AN INDIAN JOURNEY

ing for escapades raise their lustful heads, and the moonlight throws a veil over the sober significance of things.

It had grown darker as I strolled onwards. Varicoloured lights streamed through the open doorways; the streets were narrower in this quarter, and the passers-by were fewer. From time to time I heard steps drawing near, and suddenly the sound would cease as soon as the muffled nocturnal figure had passed me; the wayfarer would stand looking after me inquisitively, or perhaps scenting the chance of plunder, being allured by an intimation of the restless uncertainty which had seized me and was driving me forth through the night. For a moment I was oppressed by a sense of peril, for I knew that this part of the town was dangerous; but then I realised that life, heretofore so greatly prized, had become a matter of indifference to me. I was concerned about other things. The reign of the night was dominant, of the night on earth and of the night within my disquieted soul, which was filled with longing for the mystical day of its transmigration.

The door of a wooden house stood ajar, and when I pushed it open I looked into a narrow passage which was dimly lighted by a greenish paper lantern. The bare walls on either side of this lantern were hung with mirrors, so that the dim and flickering aspect of the quiet interior was reflected a thousandfold and transformed into a domain of magical extent. From within could be faintly heard the strumming of a stringed instrument, like a mandoline but much less lively in tone, interrupted now and again by the sustained notes of a wind instrument, probably a flute.

AN INDIAN JOURNEY

The air was laden with a heavy, sweetish odour, like that of fermenting honey or of some intoxicating drug that was being smoked; it issued through the gap of a pair of red curtains in the background, as if from the split in an over-ripe fruit.

When I had been standing for a little while in this entry, listening, the low curtain was drawn back, and an old woman advanced towards me with a hesitant tread and apparently much surprised. She was withered, and in the pale light of the paper lantern her grey hair was lustreless. A yellow cloth was wound round her toga-fashion, so that her shoulders and arms, and her legs from the knees downwards, were bare. When she had recovered from her astonishment, she smiled at me with that impersonal cordiality characteristic of those whose hospitable friendliness is the outcome of profession or custom, and, after a searching glance at my European attire, invited me to enter. She said a phrase or two which I did not understand, but which were obviously words of welcome. When I advanced confidently, her subserviency was redoubled, and as we went upstairs in a red half-light, she positively grovelled in front of me; I seemed always to see her face close to mine while the rest of her body was farther up the stairs. She looked round at me with an enticing leer. From somewhere came the tinkling of a bell. In a maze I followed, neither boldly nor cautiously, practically without thought of what was happening or might happen. Life was of little account.

We reached a door flush with the top of the staircase,

AN INDIAN JOURNEY

a door covered with many-hued paper. It opened easily and silently at the touch of the old woman's withered hand.

"Enter, Sahib," she said in Hindustani, pressing to one side against the partition, which yielded before her. I had a strong impression that we were being watched. Cautiously now, therefore, I felt my way into a low-ceilinged chamber, faintly illuminated with a bluish, misty light. At first I could make out nothing beyond the faint gleam of a lantern, the hangings on the wall with their dim but motley colours, and a few unfamiliar ornaments. The air was full of a soft but intoxicating and oppressive smell of withered jasmine and of opium.

I followed my guide through this room into a second, which was even smaller and darker. Here, at first, I could discern nothing but a wide couch, raised barely a foot from the floor, covered with gay rugs and skins. When, in accordance with the old woman's wishes, I had seated myself on this couch, she bowed many times, saying in broken English as she sidled out of the room:

"I will fetch Goy for you, Sahib. You will be delighted with her."

When I nodded, and uttered a word or two of assent, she laughed, well content to be understood. She felt she had convinced me that she was a person of refinement, and she was anxious to do nothing likely to disturb this impression.

Left to myself, I scarcely troubled to examine my surroundings. Everything must happen as had been written for this night. A greenish lantern hung close to the ceiling. I could see a small, round table, with incredibly thin legs. On the table stood a brass tray, inlaid with red and blue lacquer, and spread with dried fruits, tobacco, bhang, and betel. Now that my eyes had become accustomed to the faint light, I was able, when the door opened, to see with the lucidity of a vision the girl who entered the room and closed and bolted the door behind her. She drew near with a composed and friendly manner, as if I had been an old acquaintance, and greeted me in the Canarese fashion, laying the tips of her fingers on her forehead and bowing profoundly. Except for a diaphanous wrap of smoke-tinted silk, and a narrow leathern girdle, she was completely naked. She wore grey blossoms in her black hair. The girdle was narrow, of a dull-red ochre tint, encircling her waist without constricting it, like a ring of rusty metal. Beneath it, though she looked little more than a child, projected the well-rounded and graceful hips. Into the girdle was tucked a great flower, light-blue in colour, with a golden-brown calyx. This flower stood out in pleasing contrast with the girl's bronze skin.

Save for this flower and the lithe girlish body, all my surroundings had the strange, arresting consciousness in colour, aspect, and movement, which can only be imparted by the tradition of centuries.

I do not know whether I understood everything the child said to me on that memorable night, but I know that she and I understood one another.

In this sequestered spot, with its odours, filled with the living charm of the girl, all the petty interests and desires which disintegrate and oppress our lives, seemed to have vanished. There was but one goal for our blood.

AN INDIAN JOURNEY

"Shall I dance?" asked Goy. "Tell me what you would like me to do."

She danced beneath the greenish moon of the lantern which lighted my little world—a world full of sultriness and silence. The silence was broken only by the sound of the dancer's soft feet upon the mat. When I closed my eyes, I felt as if these feet were dancing gently upon my heart, the very source of my life. Each time I reopened my eyes, Goy's girlish form blossomed anew before my sight. It remained strange to me, changing continually like a landscape which we speed through in imagination. Then the sound of the dancing ceased, and she smiled at me with an expression simultaneously wise, childlike, and passionate.

"Will you not give me your orders, Sahib?" said Goy, so slowly that I felt as if my heart were standing still beneath the unexpressed implications of her question; and yet, behind her submissiveness, there lurked, guidelessly, a happy consciousness of power. Now, looking like a great golden cat in the strange light from the lantern, she leapt softly on to the couch beside me. With a thoughtful mien, she took a cigarette paper, crumbled tobacco and bhang, and, when she added a little opium, suddenly to my imagination she was transmuted into a goddess bringing slumber in her hands.

Like most women of the East, Goy had been trained to the uses of a kind of love which is the outcome of a sinister sensuality: and yet all her doings lay under the spell of an innocence which produced the impression of chastity. Goy did her duty, and no conscience such as dwells within

AN INDIAN JOURNEY

our breasts interfered with her fidelity to the only pleasure which she knew and gave.

I inhaled the smoke deeply and eagerly, so that more and more my senses were numbed. The girl did not let a moment pass in which she did not seem to be giving herself. Her aspect was continually changing. She did not surrender one of her secrets without giving me an inkling that another still remained to be disclosed.

"Forget life," she said with gentle reproof, apparently rendered a little uneasy by my backwardness. "Don't you think me beautiful?"

"You are lovely, Goy; the loveliest girl I have ever seen."

"Oh no," she answered thoughtfully. "Fair girls are far lovelier than I am."

When I made no answer, she looked at me with her large, childlike eyes, and smiled. Her nails were stained red. Her hands were exquisitely cared for, and so, indeed, was her whole body.

"People do not lay aside falsehood with their garments," said Goy. "I believe in nothing, save only love and its pleasures."

Her meaning was clear to me. As she spoke, she stood there tenderly offering herself to me, holding out her arms as if she were offering a cup. Her head was between me and the lantern, so that her form seemed to be framed in a magical border of light. But her words appealed to me in an unforeseen way; they took on a lustre of their own, and became enkindled for a distant journey.

Goy tried to read my thoughts in my face.

AN INDIAN JOURNEY

"Forget," she said. "What need to think? Here there is neither time, nor day, nor night."

"And yet, mistress of this little eternity, is not life longer than youth?"

"No," said Goy confidently, and her smile had in it something incredibly convincing. "For you men it may be so, but it is not so for us girls. An old woman is worse than a squeezed mango. When the limbs wither, hope withers too, for the blood loses the voice to which the course of the world renders obedience. No child will be my delight."

"What can I do for you, Goy? Take all that I have!"

"I take nothing," answered the girl. "I have never taken anything. That is for the old woman to do. Tell me that I am beautiful and that I have made you happy."

"You are very beautiful."

"That is all you say to me, so you are ungrateful. Or perhaps you are one of those who can never forget themselves—who seem to themselves so important, so important!"

She drew close to me, gazing into my eyes. Then she gently stroked my cheek, sighed deeply as if in sympathy, and bowed her head.

I closed my eyes. The fresh flower in her girdle brushed my face, and for a moment I felt as if it were pressing cold against my forehead.

"What sort of people do you mean?" I enquired.

Fleetingly it seemed as though the iridescent intoxication were vanishing, as clouds are driven before the wind. Goy meditated a while, and smiled sadly, as if she thought my case hopeless. Then, raising her hand to my brow, she tapped my temples with her fingers, and said:

"The cold fire there! It is stronger than all other flames, and seems brighter. It fights against the warmth of the heart, and has quenched the fires of many hearts. Such as you must always move from one to another. He who wishes to make of all obstacles, means to his ends, knows no rest, for the world is full of obstacles. What goal do you seek? Our sages laugh at you. Forget! Forget!"...

When I left the house, the sunlight leapt on me like a beast of prey. I staggered, feeling my way along the wall, until at length, and slowly, I recovered my self-command. I did not know how long a time had elapsed. Thus must the world have seemed to Lazarus when a god had summoned him back to life. By degrees I recalled the details of my experience, as one recalls a dream after waking from deep slumber. . . .

Perchance no more had happened, than that an avaricious old woman had misled me, and that a depraved child had shared my bed. But since I have no dread of either avarice or depravity, I was little concerned. It mattered not what these incidents might be worth in the censorious eyes of earthly justice; to me the vital matter was, how they appeared to my own eyes.

But life clouds our vision with dreams, laughter, and tears.

By degrees I became increasingly aware that my perceptions were concentrated upon that strange flower, and upon its brilliant blue, which appeared to expand before my gaze with a quiet dominance. At length I seemed to awaken in a new existence. My limbs were weighted as with an infinite fatigue, while my eyes were unsteady and stupefied, as if taken prisoner by the radiant azure of my dream flower, which now disclosed itself to be an unending blue wall. With painful effort, I endeavoured to understand this blue wall. Then I suddenly caught sight of my hand lying on my knee. It looked like a foreign object, emaciated and quite white. I tried to raise it, and it obeyed me. The indescribable thrills of an entirely new life made my limbs quiver. These thrills started from the seat of consciousness, and moved like shafts of light through my veins, resembling wayward sparks, hot and cold. I sighed profoundly, and distinctly recall saying out loud:

"This cannot be the old life."

Thereupon Panya appeared from behind a white pillar which was between me and the blue wall, and stood staring at me. He looked extraordinarily unreal, as if he were floating in the air. My thought was, "Hullo, there is a brown man with a white turban."

"Sahib!" he cried, as he looked into my eyes, "Sahib speak!"

"Where are we, Panya?" I asked feebly. "What's happened to the time, Panya?"

The boy stared at me uncomprehendingly. A fresh anxiety was obvious in his face, but this waned as he continued to look at me.

"Sahib, speak good words to me," he begged, at once dubiously and hopefully.

AN INDIAN JOURNEY

Then I realised that my questions had been in German, so I repeated them in English.

Instead of answering, Panya uttered a loud cry, fell upon his knees and embraced mine. Sobbing, he stammered:

"Sahib, you will live!"

"Where have we got to, Panya? What on earth is that blue wall?"

Panya rose with a happy laugh, moved to one side and said:

"That is the sea. We are high in the hills, and you are looking down on the sea. We carried you here from the swamps, marching for two days and two nights without stopping to sleep, and hardly resting at all until we reached the fresh air and quiet. Look round. Look at the forest! This is the abandoned bungalow of an English farm. We had to drive out the monkeys which had taken possession of the house."

He paused and looked at me once more. Then he went on:

"Oh, Sahib, now you have come to yourself again. Sense has returned to your eyes and your words, and joy was returned to my breast."

As I watched Panya weeping, I understood that he was speaking the truth, and that, from the realm of fever poisons, my spirit had come back into the world of reality. Then I saw Guru squatting on the ground a little way off, staring at me aloofly with his huge dark eyes. Never shall I forget his expression.

Not for some days, and then only snatches, did I learn

all that had happened, for Panya kept everything from me until I questioned him point blank. Most of our baggage had been lost, for my own people had to look after me, and no porters were obtainable. Panya had brought along little else than food, the boxes containing those things on which I set the greatest store, my weapons, and one of the tents. The day before I came to myself, Pasha and a coolie had set out to retrieve anything that might still be worth retrieving, and to see that what could not be brought to the bungalow at once should be housed in a native village. But Panya had little hope that anything would be recovered, and he expected the monsoon to burst at any moment. During the hot noon hours he would sit silently beside my reclining chair, watching the sky to seaward, and the wide blue plains, which from this altitude appeared as flat as a sheet of metal. Sometimes they were overhung by a fine, grey haze. But apart from this anxiety concerning the monsoon, whose gravity I well understood, another trouble weighed on the boy's mind. This was obvious to me, but I would not question him. Not until I lighted my first cigar, did Panya say with a melancholy smile:

"Now you will be strong enough to bear the worst."

Elijah had been carried off by a panther.

VII ····· IN THE HILLS ····· VII

PANYA explored the ruinous house afresh where with considerable difficulty a room had been arranged so that it could be closed at night.

"Will you stay here, Sahib, until the rains?" he asked.

I knew that this would not do at all, and that we should be lost if the monsoon burst before we had left the mountains. I vainly endeavoured to estimate the time that had elapsed since our departure from Cannanore. It might have been four, five, or six months.

Gurumahu came one morning to report that he was suffering from homesickness. He would leave us with a heavy heart, but if he was to reach his village before the rains began, it was time for him to start.

I bestowed on him an old nickel watch which had been specially made for tropical use. Doubtless this was not a very magnificent parting gift, although the watch could tick vigorously, and in dry weather might actually go. Guru, however, accepted it with enthusiasm. Henceforward he would be able to learn from it whatever his heart desired to know: the seasons, the direction of the wind, and the course of the stars.

Many of the necessaries of life were lacking to us. Panya's troubled expression of countenance frightened me out of the illusion I had begun to cherish, that the cool and invigorating hill air, in conjunction with the natural high spirits of a convalescent, justified a cheerful outlook upon the future. Most of the baggage had been rescued. The white ants, however, had wrought havoc among our food supply. Still, there were not many mouths to feed. Besides myself, Panya, and Pasha, there were only two porters from South Canara. These latter, with great expenditure of labour, and often at the hazard of their lives, would from time to time procure rice and fruit from the nearest jungle village. The natives had realised that we were dependent upon their aid, and consequently my store of money was rapidly melting away. Panya was outraged by these exactions. He muttered imprecations against the extortioners, and more than once he vowed that he would burn their village over their heads. My equanimity led him to take me seriously to task.

"Sahib, you are a great lord. You can do whatever you please, but you do nothing. The days pass one after another like waves breaking on the shore. They leave no trace, and each day is like the one before. How can anyone make his living in such a fashion? When we were in Anantapur you used to mock at the Brahmins for lying in the sun all day, and eating the temple rice as they are privileged to do. Now you are as idle as they. Formerly you would write in your books about everything you saw, and you used to ask me many questions. But now you do not even do that, and the books are all burned."

This last was a great distress to Panya, for he knew that a good deal had been said about him in these notebooks, and he had been pluming himself upon the fame that awaited him in the west, the land of the white lords. As far as that matter was concerned, I laughed at him;

but he was in the right of it about the monsoon, so at length I made up my mind to take the shortest route to Mangalore, and to spend the rainy season in the safe shelter of that ancient city.

At the bottom of my heart, nevertheless, when I meditated this plan, I realised all that I was giving up, all that I should leave behind me. I felt that never again should I have experiences resembling my recent ones in respect of light and freedom. Consequently I postponed our departure from day to day, although all my life in the hills was spent in that condition of cloudy uncertainty and

AN INDIAN JOURNEY

unaccountable restlessness which is apt to seize us in beautiful surroundings when we have already made up our minds to leave.

Never shall I forget Gong. He is probably dead by now, for he was not in his first youth when I made his acquaintance. His mistrust of me was never completely overcome. He was one of those hill monkeys of India, which are more imposing than their brethren of the jungle. They have different ways, but it would not be true to say that they have better manners.

To this companion of mine during the early morning hours I gave the name of Gong on account of his extraordinarily hideous voice, the tones of which resembled the noise made by throwing a rusty old tin kettle against a stone wall. Fortunately he had not much to say, but he was greatly interested in all my doings. He had obviously made up his mind to enjoy some signal experience before departing this life. Having pitched upon me as the person most likely to put him in the way of such happenings, he came to spend his mornings beneath the tall latania and tamarind trees overlooking the house.

Not wishing to miss the coolest hours, it was my custom to rise as soon as the distant sea began to silver in the twilight. Through the bars of the window grating came this pale light reflected from the waters, hardly distinguishable from moonlight. From the landward side were now heard the first calls of the birds of prey, as they circled round the crags already standing out clear against the dawn. An hour must pass ere the rays of the sun would reach our highland. At first, far to the west, I could see the sunlight sparkling on the water. Eastwards, the crags would now show golden edges as they thrust upwards against the pale-blue background of the sky. Morning after morning, their radiant stillness was a fresh delight to me, and the peace with which they filled my soul lasted far on into the day—for here there was nothing to ruffle my tranquillity. Those only can understand nature who learn to know her in such a manner and under such conditions; for, like all that is great, she demands from us a limitless self-surrender before she will reveal herself to us fully.

At this hour, Gong would take up his station in one of the trees close to the house, usually upon a thick branch near the ground. To be ready for any emergency, he would keep one hand upon a higher branch, and if my gun were within reach, nothing at first would persuade him to linger. I do not know when or how he had made acquaintance with this weapon, but I am certain that the monkeys had known me and watched me far longer than I had known and watched them.

At the outset a great troop of his companions was in attendance. It was easy to observe them, for the trees were widely spaced, and the monkeys could only progress from tree to tree by way of the ground. One day, Gong departed from the custom of his tribe, for he remained seated as I drew near. This brought me to a standstill, so astonished was I to notice that he did not immediately make off. He was sitting on one of the thick lower branches, holding on with all four, as if wishing to keep

AN INDIAN JOURNEY

himself from taking to flight. Trembling, and raising his eyebrows, he contemplated me with a mixture of curiosity, spitefulness, and fear.

In general, my experience of animals has convinced me that they do not try to work us a mischief unless we take the lead. Perhaps my conviction depends upon the fact that during boyhood I was never hurt by a dog, a horse, or a cat, although I cannot venture to say that I always refrained from teasing. An additional reason may perhaps be that a sense of superiority is distasteful to me. Of all the sentiments that can be aroused through companionship with other living creatures—men or beasts—the most offensive to me is that sort of exultation. I am ever wont to fancy that those who are most ready to assume such a pose are in reality the most paltry of mortals. The very essence of respect for living creatures is that one should not set oneself apart from them. We must concede rights to others, and we should claim rights only when our leadership is essential to the common welfare. Among all the voices of life which stress our emotions during our brief earthly span, the sighs of the oppressed have ever been, for my ears, the most conspicuous tones—like a clamorous motif in a tempestuous piece played on the organ. Since it is equally repugnant to me to be compelled to give sympathy and to receive it, my only resource has been to regard the life of all living things as a natural expression, and as having rights co-equal with those of my own.

When Gong remained seated on his branch, though his fellow monkeys had fled, I could discern in his face, as I

AN INDIAN JOURNEY

slowly drew near, the tension of one whose heart palpitates as he see-saws betwixt fear and curiosity. Suddenly, however, it occurred to him that there was a third possibility, and he tried to intimidate me, to prove to me that he was a person of importance, with forest rights of his own. First drawing his head down between his shoulders, he then stretched it forwards with a jerk, at the same time shaking the branch on which he was sitting, and swaying his body to and fro with all his might, as if about to make a savage onslaught. From his pouting lips came a sound hard to describe. You can produce something like it by pressing a lamp chimney to your mouth, and by trumpeting through this, in chest notes and with a tone of fierce conviction, "Great Scott!"

The effect was so comical that I burst out laughing, and slapped my thigh resoundingly. For a moment Gong was disconcerted; but then, deciding that my gestures were friendly advances, he imitated them to the best of his ability. His eyes, however, retained their serious expression, and his forehead was still puckered.

On this occasion, and thenceforward, we showed our mutual sympathy by imitating one another as well as we could. Amusing as we doubtless were to one another in this respect, it remains somewhat distressing to me when I recall how greatly I fell short of Gong as a mimic.

In the course of our acquaintanceship it became plain to me that Gong was much vexed whenever I failed to put in an appearance, and that he was honestly pleased by my little attentions. Perhaps he may have thought that I reciprocated this feeling. He was anxious to learn, and was eager to understand anything within his powers. Even though at times he could get no further than outward mimicry, the wish for a neighbourly approximation was manifest on both sides.

It is true that he would never let me come quite close to him on the physical plane. My distance was five or six paces. As soon as I attempted to approach any nearer, he would wave me away regretfully, and would seize a higher branch, as a hint of what would happen were I to come closer.

During the progress of our friendship, Gong learned everything concerning a man's activities which can be learned simply by inspection from a distance. He had put my sun-helmet on his head; he had used my pocket handkerchief: and he knew the functions of a knife. He had fluttered the leaves of my notebooks; he had swung in my hammock: and he could imitate the movements of putting on and taking off a coat so perfectly that the onlooker might have imagined he had worn clothing all his life.

We were not always entirely pleased with one another, for Gong knew no limits to his endeavours to be like me. I was nettled at times by his mimicry, which made my own doings appear ludicrous to me. I felt that he was mocking me. Indeed, it became necessary to consider how Gong could be unschooled of some of his acquirements, for it grew plainer from day to day that he, and his companions as well, no longer took me seriously, and that they failed to show me the respect to which I deemed myself entitled. These monkeys positively laughed whenever I appeared. Sometimes they closed in upon me in serried ranks, in

AN INDIAN JOURNEY

order to make fun of everything I did. They nudged one another to draw attention to me, rubbing their grey hands gleefully, and smacking their thighs. They chattered in all possible tones, while begrudging one another some trifle which an instant before they had been willing to share. All the time their demeanour was so self-important that it would have seriously annoyed a more even-tempered person than myself.

I was never alone now, for my train followed me wherever I went. Respect for the gun lessened as the days passed, for the monkeys had realised that it was used only to shoot birds and four-footed game, and that the great race of quadrumana was quite immune from danger. Whenever some little creature had fallen to my marksmanship, they would wait until I had laid down the weapon, and would then come close to me in crowds, with gestures showing their conviction that I had them to thank for my success.

What annoyed me more than anything else was their forgetfulness. It was really scandalous to see how at one moment they would make a tremendous fuss about something, and a moment later would let it slip from memory as if there had never been such a thing in the world. New whims took hold of them and passed in an instant, and in each fresh pose they would insist on being taken no less seriously than in the last. After a time I came to regard myself as a visitor in some foreign town, an eccentric tolerated by the citizens because he was a source of amusement to them. My observations of animals and the world were confusing my judgment.

AN INDIAN JOURNEY

I recounted my troubles to Panya.

"Monkeys!" he said. "Who is to bother about monkeys? But as for you, Sahib, if you see a cricket you grow thoughtful. You start talking to the insect, and behave as if it were answering you. Anyone who keeps company with monkeys begins to think his own shadow has grown foolish—and who can catch a shadow?"

"I want to catch Gong," I answered.

Panya reflected. "When I was a boy I often caught monkeys with a noose. If the monkey you want to catch knows you and has confidence in you, you will be able to catch him easily. All you need do is to show him how to get into a noose and get out again. He will learn only the first half of the trick, and if you are quick enough you can seize him. But you must keep his attention fixed on your left hand, and with your right hand seize him by the scruff of the neck before he realises what you are doing. Old monkeys will bite as long as they think there is a chance of escape. They give up biting when they see it is no good."

It was a splendid idea. Next morning I took a stout hempen cord and greased it. When my troublesome friends came to greet me, I made a noose, and ensnared myself in all sorts of ways, now on the arm, now on the neck, and so on, especially drawing Gong's attention to what I was doing. His fellow monkeys scattered in alarm, for these gestures were new to them, but Gong watched me with a serious mien. As soon as I thought that I had given enough demonstrations, I opened the noose to a suitable width, withdrew to a little distance, and

AN INDIAN JOURNEY

lay down on the grass to watch the success of the manœuvre.

But Gong remained quietly seated on his branch, raising his eyebrows, and looking by turns at the noose and at me. Next he made an angry grimace, and, thrusting out his head at me, contemptuously exclaimed, "Great Scott!", and turned away to look at the view.

I heard Panya laughing behind me, and instantly resolved to slay him.

"Sahib," said he, "this monkey knows what a noose is. He knows men, and that is why he lets you come so close to him."

"What are you laughing at?" I exclaimed. "Who gave you leave to laugh?"

"How can I help laughing?" said Panya.

Then I saw the joke too, and laughed in unison.

The green wilderness of the jungle in the plains steamed in the morning sunshine, and was often veiled in mist until noon. In the fresh hill air, I found it difficult at times to understand how I could have endured the air of the lowlands for so long. At night the panther would occasionally prowl even on the veranda, driven by hunger out of the arid uplands of the neighbourhood. The wild beasts in general had withdrawn into the jungle from the parched open country; and when in the afternoon, gun on shoulder, I left the woodland to walk over the bare hills, the only animals I encountered were jackals and hyenas. But they always slunk away out of range. I sometimes thought I was going to have a shot at a jackal, but the grey-brown tint of this animal matches so perfectly with the colour of the ground, that hardly had I caught sight of the graceful little head, with its long, pointed ears, when the creature would vanish, swallowed up by its surroundings.

Shortly before we left, I shot my first panther. One moonlit night Panya came into my room and called me. Behind him stood Pasha, tall and straight. Besides the moonlight, there played on his figure from beneath, the light of the fire which was burning in the enclosure.

"Sahib," said Panya, "the panther is so hungry that he is eating the fire. We can't drive him away, and it is impossible to get any sleep."

The news was welcome. I took up my gun and told Panya to quench the flames. The porters were away in the plains, having gone to buy rice and fowls. They were not expected back until the next evening. I loaded both barrels with ball, and placed my revolver handy. There was no glass in the window, which was protected merely by thick staves. Some of these had been renewed by Panya, but they would not have withstood a serious attack. I took up my position in the shadow, and we waited.

Pasha lay down in the corner of the room, and soon I heard him snoring. Panya remained close by me, having armed himself with the longest knife in our outfit, and with a bill-hook. He brandished it as if he were an Indian chief, grinning with excitement, and then began so admirable an imitation of the bleating of a goat that for the first time I fully realised that we were waiting here for the great beast of prey.

Perhaps an hour had slipped away, and I was beginning

AN INDIAN JOURNEY

to lose patience, when suddenly the moonlight was eclipsed. Strangely enough, the last thing I thought of for a time was the panther, especially since all was now still, for the beast must have got wind of us when he made his last movement. At length, I perceived the huge cat just in front of me. Big as he was, he was smaller than I had pictured him, and in that light almost colourless; but I could distinctly make out the supple vigour of the beautifully curved back, and I could see the splendid cat-like head, which was turned towards me with half-opened mouth. At this moment there came a sound which made my blood run cold. It was a hissing snarl, loud and clear, expressing mingled anger and dread—a sound that paralysed the will. I remembered that I had heard this hideous and terrifying snarl at the zoological gardens in my childhood, when one of the keepers had passed close by the bars of the tiger's cage. It was true that now likewise I was separated from the beast of prey by a grating, but the fierceness of his voice made him seem so close that even the strongest of iron bars would hardly have inspired me with confidence.

I cannot now recall whether I already had my gun at my shoulder, or whether I shouldered it at the last instant, but I know that I took aim without feeling the slightest confidence in the effect of the discharge. I fired between the beast's eyes, which I could plainly distinguish, relying more upon the natural tendency of my arms to give the right direction to the barrels, than upon the sight. I fired both barrels in brief and perhaps too rapid succession.

I heard a noise on the floor of the veranda, as if the

beast had leapt down from the roof. An instant later, one of the staves in the window snapped like a pipe-stem beneath a terrible blow from the creature's paw. Then all was still on the veranda, as we listened to the echoes of the shots reverberating from crag to crag and rolling along the valleys, to die away finally in the distance of the moonlit night, like the clamour of two brothers fleeing before the hunters.

After this, the first definite sensation that brought me to myself was a pain in the hand with which I was grasping my revolver as firmly as if my life depended on it. I could not recollect having taken it up; but now, drawing a deep breath, I relaxed my grip, and realised that I was shaking all over as if in the cold stage of fever. Subsequently, in Canara and Mysore, I shot many panthers; some in ricefields, some in rocky ravines, and some that were crouching on branches: but never again, even when the danger was far greater, did I feel anything like my present sense of horror and helplessness. An inadequate protection will often make us far more anxious than the certainty of having to face danger without any protection at all—and this not only where panthers are concerned! Moreover, when for months in the darkness of the night one has been aware of the beast's proximity, it is a rather alarming experience to encounter one of these great cats face to face for the first time, so that the imagination, ever busily at work, has created a fabulous monster even more formidable than the panther is in reality.

In truth panthers are timid creatures. They hardly ever attack human beings, not even children, unless in an extremity of hunger or when they turn at bay. When they are satiated, they always avoid the neighbourhood of man, and they kill only what they actually need. In Malabar I talked with a number of herdsmen concerning tigers and panthers, and all of them agreed that these cats were easily satisfied. In ordinary circumstances the panther will carry off one goat from the flock, eat his fill, and generously leave the remains for the hyenas which are nearly always to be found in his train. He will only attack these hyenas when he is positively famished.

Tales of tigers are numerous and conflicting. They must be accepted with caution, for the natives have such a superstitious dread of the tiger that hardly any of them can distinguish between fact and allegory. So persistent is the awe inspired by the tiger, that in many provinces this beast of prey has the same name as Satan, the Evil One. We can understand how this comes about when we realise that few of the natives are armed, and that their leaf huts afford no adequate protection against nocturnal raids. Among all the legends of the tiger, this one is certainly true, that a tiger which has tasted human flesh is rarely content with other food. A man-eating tiger will arouse panic throughout a whole countryside.

In the twilight of morning we found the slaughtered panther among the aloes. The ground had been trampled and torn in his death agony. But the great beast now lay quiet, looking almost peaceful, and with no obvious sign of injury. On close examination, I found that he had been hit by only one of the bullets, which had entered behind the ear, traversing the neck and breaking the spine.

AN INDIAN JOURNEY

The eyes were closed, which is rare in a slaughtered beast. The muzzle, beautifully moulded, had a pained and almost tender expression, the jaws being slightly parted, as if in a last sigh. The thorny, bluish-green leaves of the aloes contrasted with the yellow tint of the panther's fur, the colour-scheme being strangely harmonious, and seeming peculiarly appropriate to these Indian surroundings. I shall never forget the picture, which is so strongly impressed upon my mind because now for the first time I felt that I had fully grasped the indescribable charm of India, which in all its significance and peculiarity can be conveyed neither by the brush of the painter nor by the words of the poet.

Panya was silent all the morning. A great lord of the hills was dead. My own thoughts were troubled throughout the day. At times I felt as if a heinous and stupid act of violence had been committed, as if I had done a wrong to the splendour and multiformity of creation, some of whose most perfect work is being effaced slowly by the extermination of the great cats of India.

VIII • THE THRONE OF THE SUN • VIII

 WAS kept awake sometimes by the moonlight, which walked like the soothsaying spectre of the everlasting chill of death along the crumbling walls that sheltered me from the dangers of the outer world. Then there would dawn in my breast the longing to scale the heights which the rising sun tinted every morning with ruddy gold. I desired to gaze from that cool and lofty tranquillity over the Indian land beyond the mountains, there to relive in imagination the days I had known before I came to Cannanore.

Panya stared at me in amazement when I told him of my new plans. Dumping the kettle heavily on the fire so that the sparks flew, he contemplated me for a while with an expression like that of those who despair of carrying their point, and yet cannot conceal their wish to do so. Then he said resignedly:

"After all, it does not matter whether we come to grief there or here."

AN INDIAN JOURNEY

This confirmed me in my resolve, for, like all those who are at once wayward and obstinate, I often yield to the impulse to use as a springboard any lath which chance has thrown under my feet. Of course he who would take such ventures must be able to jump, and "ability to jump" is in essence what most people term "having luck." There is no such thing as "having luck." What is called luck is intimately associated with adroitness, just as ill-luck is intimately associated with maladroitness. Nor does this truth relate only to outward happenings. Ill-luck—or unhappiness—within the mind is in the last analysis maladroitness, though in a far more exalted sense, whose significance finds expression in the ordering of the universe.

I did not trouble Panya with these reflections, but watched him as he ran hither and thither, bustling about with the furniture in a way which showed plainly that no real purpose underlay his zeal. We can often note that persons who are out of temper are prone to move objects of small weight from one place to another, and then perhaps to move them back again. The inference is justified that the thoughts and intentions of such persons are vacillating in like fashion, and that their doings are the outcome of a hidden tendency to harmonise the movements of body and mind. As I looked on at Panya's futile activities, I was reminded of my father's ways when for one reason or another he had occasion to show that his views and mine were at odds. I am sorry to say that this usually happened when we were at dinner, for at other times I avoided as far as possible sitting in his company for any considerable time. At dinner, then, I would watch him as

AN INDIAN JOURNEY

he fidgeted with knife or fork, with salt-cellar or napkin ring, shifting them alternately from right to left and from left to right of his plate. We used to have on the dinner table a knife-sharpener made of corundum, a cylinder of round, dark stone of about the size of a stick of asparagus, with a polished hard-wood handle. If my father happened to be laying down the law with particular emphasis at a time when he was holding the knife-sharpener, the results were usually disastrous to the latter, for, resistant as corundum is to steel, it is apt to be broken by a blow on the dinner table.

Such an accident would increase my father's annoyance with me and would bring my mother into the dispute. But as far as I was concerned it tended to elate me, and would make me feel—perhaps with good reason—that my father's view of my character would have been much less harsh had the family knife-sharpener been of steel.

My reverie led me to tell Panya what I thought about knife-sharpeners, and the utterly unexpected expression of my opinion on this point brought him to his senses sufficiently to induce him to bring me my morning tea.

He drank tea with me, as our custom was, squatting opposite me in the sunlight and plucking gloomily at his turban. For some weeks past he had worn, in addition to this head-dress, nothing more than a loin-cloth, but even in the greatest heat he would never discard his heavy turban. One of his peculiarities was that when at the outset he had been antagonistic to some plan of mine, he would be all the more eager to carry it out from the moment he realised that my mind was made up. In both his opposition and his subsequent fervour I recognised the working of an honest affection, and I never think of him without a pang, for our parting was one of the greatest losses of my life. The harmony of our relation may have been based upon his conviction that the superiority of my race had the force of a law of nature. Since he was imbued with this feeling, his devotion to me had nothing base about it, but had rather the exaltation of a religious sentiment. To-day, in Malabar, he is tilling his rice-fields beside the Purrha, close to which the hut of his fathers stands in a shady palm grove. He had been compelled to leave his home and to take service with the white men because his brothers had played the spendthrift in the great towns. My last gift to him was the repurchase of this small ancestral estate; my one regret is that I could never make him understand that his gifts to me were greater and more imperishable.

When we had drunk our tea, he angrily exclaimed:

"But Pasha will stay here!"

He continued to keep up the pretence that the proposed expedition was out of the question, until, forgetting himself once more, he said:

"The climb will take three days or three nights, but the descent will take only half the time. Did you think it was going to take longer?"

My estimate had been much the same.

Panya looked at the hilltops. They were flooded with light; their serene solitude was illumined with an unwonted brilliance; the eagles circling round the crags sparkled as if their wings were made of gold.

"In the freshness of the heights, dreams have long abiding," he mused.

"Listen, Panya. He only who has learned to love the beauty of the world, has really made the world his own in his brief earthly sojourn. In this sense, God has given us the world; he has dealt with us as if the world were his gift to us."

Panya smiled in answer. At such moments I felt like hugging him.

"No ill will befall you, Sahib," he said quietly, and as if speaking to himself.

I do not know whether his confidence arose from his belief in God's aid or in his own. But of this much I am certain, that rarely has a human companionship made me happier than his. How can anyone aid us more effectively than by expressing his belief in our own powers?

Next day, therefore, we started on our climb before dawn, when it was still quite dark, and the stars were shining above the blue mountain tops. We heard the cicadas singing here and there as we stepped out through the arid herbage beneath and between the tall latania trees, which were here widely separated one from another. From time to time a monkey, awakened by our footfalls, scolded us overhead; or we would flush a bird which would rise with a loud warning cry, notifying our presence to unsuspecting nature, whose solitude here had not presumably been troubled for ages by the tread of man. It was calm and still. Panya had nothing to say, and as I moved onwards, spellbound by the encompassing solitude, it seemed to me

AN INDIAN JOURNEY

at times as if—an alien third—I were watching our two puny figures as they strode across the titanic greyish-green waves of the upland landscape, in the half light beneath the trees and the stars.

We were rash to have set off without torches, for in the early morning at this season of the year the panther is at his boldest as he slinks towards his lair in the gloom after a night's vain hunting. So bright, however, was the starlight that we could see to a considerable distance, and I had my gun with me. Panya walked beside me without speaking, treading lightly and holding his head erect, radiating energy and joy. I felt that he was akin to all the life of his native land, and I shared in the harmony of his soul as if his country had been mine also.

Of a sudden he began to sing softly, still keeping his eyes fixed on the heights, and as completely absorbed in his own thoughts as if he had been alone. The hum of his voice and the monotonous rhythm of his song reminded me of the singing of the priests whose temple in Cannanore had stood in the palm grove behind my garden. In an instant I was transported from the free heights and the cool air into the tropical plains, so that I felt as if the sultry vapours of the luxuriant vegetation were steaming around me.

A little later, when I raised my eyes after we had left the woodland, I was startled to see a jagged line of flame-red light running horizontally high above us, and sundering the heavens in twain. In absolute stillness, this red band zig-zagged along the crest of the mountains. Behind the heights the sun had risen! Turning in surprise, I

AN INDIAN JOURNEY

saw behind us the land beneath the starry blue of the vanishing night; and beyond the land, on the distant sea, was a dull, silvery sheen. As between two heavens, one of blood and one of silver, my fascinated heart was pulsing on the wide dusky-green waves of earth—this heart of mine which was infinitely small and was yet the joyful fount of my immeasurable delight in being alive. Panya fell on his knees and hid his face in his hands.

An hour later, when the sun was beginning to show over the hilltops, we had got almost completely above the trees. From a shoulder, indeed, we could see on either hand in the distance the dark masses of great forests; but we soon lost sight of these, having entered a ravine to make our way upwards along the dry bed of a torrent. Ere long we realised that we were not adequately equipped for climbing one of the peaks, and Panya therefore proposed that we should make our way to the top of the nearest pass. We were able to continue afoot almost the whole of the morning, for the air was cool, and was so clear that a cloudless summer day in Germany would have seemed misty in comparison. Panya's cheerfulness made all our difficulties of little moment. He laughed again and again for no obvious reason, simply in the exuberance of his vitality, and in his delight at finding himself in this world overarched with so heavenly a blue.

Towards noon, when we had climbed much higher, we stopped to rest in the shadow of a great rock. Panya was preparing the midday meal. Suddenly, from near at hand, came a startling noise, a dull but swelling thunder. Panya

AN INDIAN JOURNEY

sprang to his feet, and, shading his eyes, looked across the shimmering upland.

"Buffaloes!" he exclaimed. "Look at the cloud rushing down the slope."

This was the first time I had seen a herd of buffaloes near at hand. The herd moved downwards like a dusky avalanche, and the earth resounded beneath the hoofs. For a moment only could I distinguish in the van one or another of the heavily-horned, swarthy heads, could make out the sheen of the huge eyes, and the waving of the manes. I did not shoot, for Panya hastily interfered when I raised my weapon. Subsequently he explained to me that the leading bull, terrified or infuriated by an attack, might have charged in our direction. We could have sought safety on the rocks, but had we failed to find a refuge in time, we should certainly have been trampled to death, for the whole herd follows the bull.

"Buffaloes will fight with the tiger," said Panya. "Even tame buffaloes are not afraid of him. If you keep buffaloes in your rice-fields, the tiger will not attack you there. The buffalo will scent the tiger long before you sight the beast, and will stand his ground, always facing the enemy with the same certainty as that with which a flag streams down the wind. Should the tiger venture a spring, he will find his death on the buffalo's horns, and you will be perfectly safe as long as you keep behind the buffalo."

The cloud of dust passed away down the valley, and the clear atmosphere was still once more. Thereupon I fell asleep, without having eaten, and Panya did not rouse me, for he knew and dreaded the power of the sun. On the

AN INDIAN JOURNEY

mountain summits in the tropics its rays are no less deadly than in the plains, although the coolness may be deceptive. White men, therefore, find it necessary to be almost more careful in the hills than in the plains to protect the head from the full force of the sun; and many have died of sunstroke because they forgot or would not believe that the sun can be dangerous when the air is cool. My sun-helmet was no longer a heavy headgear. Indeed, from day to day it grew lighter, for a number of moth-like parasites had attacked it, had made of it both their dwelling-place and their larder. Occasionally some cork dust would fall from the helmet, as an amiable reminder from nature that she allows no man to pursue his course entirely alone. Panya had employed all sorts of measures against these creatures, but they would not forsake me; and they multiplied the more vigorously, the more diligently Panya attempted to cope with them.

In a little while, from a lofty pass, I was able to look down over the expanse of country through which I had travelled before coming to Malabar. Like a troubled sea whose gigantic waves had been solidified in the midst of a storm, the vast landscape of rolling hills had borne for æons the aspect it bore now, with never a sign of man's handiwork. In the remoter distance, the plateau had a light-grey sheen, and looked like the surface of a mighty ocean; but I fancied that here and there I could discern slender spires and turrets, standing out against the horizon in a way which recalled the prickles of barbed wire.

We spent the whole of the following day on the top of the pass, sheltered from the sun by a leaning rock. The silence of the heights was broken only by the cries of the eagles; and as we rested there, the figures of memory floated through my mind as if in an hour of leave-taking. From out the blue of heaven, spirits came to my spirit. To me, who yet lingered on earth, came the spirits of those who had vanished—kindred souls and alien souls, hope and destiny, friends and foes, in the world of joy and sorrow and sudden death.

In each part of the earth, death has a different visage. Nowhere are its lineaments more pompous than in Europe; but I am no longer greatly impressed by the imposing Sunday attire worn by death in my homeland. We may canonise the spectre of arbitrary power, but this does not deprive it of its dreadfulness. The cumbrously romantic conception of death which is dominant in Europe has been engendered by the church, which magnifies it to monstrous proportions for the sake of magnifying its own authority. Hence death has come to bulk so hugely in our imagination that beyond question no small proportion alike of the just and of the unjust will be most agreeably disillusioned when their hour comes.

Death is a duty, just as much as life. Each one of us will die easily or with difficulty, according as to his temperament life has been a matter of ease or difficulty; and he who has understood life, will understand death likewise. The folk of India die more easily than we; they take death more as a matter of course, and encounter it less ceremoniously; they leave the hereafter to God, and are disinclined to accept our view that at the last hour they should make themselves responsible for an orderly exit.

AN INDIAN JOURNEY

This view, the view that is termed Christian, is nowise an expression of the convictions of the guileless founder of our church, but is the outcome of the shrewd calculations of its prelates.

Slowly the sun moved along its brilliant course, and as it moved the country changed in aspect. When shall I know such days once again, days spent in perfect tranquillity, devoted to meditation and memory, filled with the sound of the eagles' war-cries? Looking down slopes glowing in the sunlight and bathed in the wonderful clarity of the ether, I became as it were intoxicated with the visions of memory, reliving in fancy all that I had seen and experienced when traversing the regions that now stretched at my feet. To the northward must lie Bijapur, the ancient royal seat, from among whose ruined palaces rose the mighty dome built by one of the erstwhile Mohammedan rulers. The interior had been lined with gold. When the eastern doors were opened, so that the light of the rising sun was reflected a thousandfold, no one could look on the splendours without being dazzled. In the centre, beneath the arched golden roof, were the thrones of the maharaja and his son Khunvar. Here the king received his guests in the angry blaze of the morning sun. The precious metal, mined from his mountains, and the heavens' light of the new day, ministered to his glory; and the bewildered friends of his realm, conducted to his throne at the moment when the sun rose, heard the ruler's greeting coming from amid a radiance before which they must fain veil their eyes and kneel humbly on the ground. It must have seemed as if heaven and earth were joining forces to exalt the power of the prince, to make his grandeur inconceivable in its immensity. Between the golden dome and the marble terrace across which newcomers were led was a sunk garden full of flowers, such flowers as bloom only in the tropics, and their fragrance was an added delight.

This lover of display was overthrown by a mightier ruler, who came from the north and destroyed the town. The slain choked the gates. The body of the fallen sultan was found slashed to pieces. When dying, he had clenched his teeth upon the ivory hilt of his sword, in his fierce unwillingness to surrender the weapon to his enemies. The body lay beneath a mountain of his dead retainers, faithful to the last. Legend tells that he was buried, as he was found, in the great mausoleum which he had built for himself according to the custom of the kings of that epoch.

These gigantic mausoleums still tower over the ruins of Bijapur, recalling mosques in their architecture and size. Indeed, religious services are still held in some of them, and Mohammedan pilgrims travel in their thousands from immense distances to visit the holy city of the dead heroes. The source of some of the stone used in the edifices is still unknown. A few of the tombstones are black slabs of a basalt-like rock, which experts believe to be of meteoric origin. The largest of the chapels is roofed by a dome from whose gallery the observer looks down dizzily upon the tombstones which appear no larger than matchboxes. So vast is the spread of the dome that the features of a person standing on the opposite side of the gallery are unrecognisable, although a whisper is plainly audible all round the circle, being conducted along the wall. It is told in story that the sultan was accustomed, in this whispering gallery, to test the fidelity of his ministers, the devotion of his guests, and the affection of his wives. Visiting the place with such persons and their intimates, he would utter provocative expressions, and would then stroll away with an affectation of indifference, to eavesdrop in another part of the gallery for the possibility of disloyal utterances. In awe of this wonder, people still tremble to-day when they meditate upon the magic power of the dead monarch.

In one of the largest of the temples I found, instead of the customary two tombstones covering the bodies of the king and queen and forming the only contents of the building, three. In this exceptional instance the king's favourite had been buried beside him and his lawful spouse, the mother of his heir. The ordinary practice was to inter beside the sultan that wife only who had given birth to the heir. The other wives and their children had no legal rights, however extensive the influence they may have used or misused.

The tenant of the third tomb had been a young woman whom the aging king had tenderly loved, but on one occasion when he returned from a campaign her enemies had been able to sow in the king's heart a suspicion that she was unfaithful. She protested her innocence, but the false witness convinced the king against his will. Torn by conflicting emotions, he conceived the idea of an ordeal which would show whether she were innocent or guilty. He led her to the topmost gallery of the mausoleum he had had built for himself. To the pair, looking down over the low

AN INDIAN JOURNEY

parapet, the great square stones of the flooring seemed no larger than the chequers on a chess-board. Now the king commanded the young woman to leap over the parapet, and she obeyed. Her loose vesture ballooned out, so that she reached the pavement uninjured. Waving a salutation to the lover who had mistrusted her, she slew herself with a dagger, and was buried with the weapon in her heart. The common people speak of her as "the alien woman," when, apprehensively, they point out her tombstone. This awe is presumably inspired by the fact that, to the oriental imagination, her deliberate choice of death, when the ordeal had proved her innocent, seems strange and inexplicable.

Profound dejection now seized the monarch. But the spirit of vengeance glowed fiercely within him, to be quieted only by death. His cruelty was atrocious. The calumniators suffered a horrible death. Thenceforward, every morning, he would test the sharpness of his scimitar on the naked back of the slave who held the stirrup for him to mount. Water-colour portraits of this ruler can be bought in Bijapur to-day. He squats on a satin cushion, with his sword across his knees. From beneath his jewelled turban, his eyes stare coldly into the distance. Strangely enough, though he held aloof from his subjects, though his glance was a terror to all, and though no maiden throughout the land was safe from his lust, rumour has it that he was more beloved than any prince who reigned before or after. His warriors are said to have gone to death at his behoof in the conviction that such a death was a sure passport to paradise, and his foes fell a prey to the

AN INDIAN JOURNEY

wrath of the people. The tale is a fresh proof of how little the popularity of a sovereign depends on his good qualities. It is the most flagrant of errors to suppose that the love of the subjects and the affability of the ruler go hand in hand.

When I entered Bijapur, death was busy in the town. We came on horseback early one morning without having heard that plague was raging there. Shortly before we reached the gate, my companion pointed to the hills adjoining the town, which were covered with tents. He suggested that we should retrace our steps; but this was impracticable, for we were short of food and water.

The presence of the camps on the heights showed us that the inhabitants had fled from the stricken city; and in the domain of the splendid ruins we found none but the dead. The horses trembled when we first encountered the repulsive, sweetish odour of putrefaction. Every time we turned a corner, numberless vultures rose heavily with hideous cries. Corpses lay in the doorways and in the streets; death stared at us from empty eye-sockets and blackened faces; our horses' hoofs became entangled in the rotting coils of human entrails which the vultures had dragged in all directions.

The light of the pitiless sun was reflected from the marble palaces; the torrid air was motionless; a couple of goats, strayed and forgotten, were wandering through the terrible desert of death amid the titanic splendours of the past. Plague had followed on the heels of famine. Still vivid in my memory are the emaciated dusky bodies, blackened by the poisons of corruption, leaning against white walls, tumbled athwart stone stairways, or recumbent on the reddish ground. Two children, who had perished in a last embrace on the edge of a temple pond, looked almost as if they had fallen asleep. There was no trace of fear or pain in their tender faces, but the eyes had been torn out, and a grey vulture was pecking at the bodies so lustily that the little heads rocked to and fro. As I drew near, the bird raised his own bald head, looking at me fiercely out of his yellow eyes, as if wondering that a living man should dare to invade his realm of death.

When the sun had set behind the sea, and when its last light had vanished across the distant water like the passing of a violent mist, Panya lighted a small fire beneath the rock that sheltered us on two sides. We had to be thrifty with the fuel, most of which Panya had collected on the way up and had carried to our lofty camp.

The night was absolutely calm; the world seemed to have died; nothing stirred, except that a couple of huge moths came to visit the fire, and the murmur of their wings filled the air until this gentler sound was drowned in Panya's snoring. In the distance I could hear the laughing of hyenas and the faint barking of jackals. Through the mist rising from the lowlands, the starlight was diffused and lustreless; but in the zenith above the rock pinnacles the stars sparkled fiercely, as if in the divine intoxication of their extra-terrestrial freedom. The waning moon was not due to rise till after midnight.

I slept but a brief span, for I did not wish to miss the sunrise. The hours of my lonely vigil on the mountains, in the silvern blue of the tropic night, have remained an inviolable possession, an investiture of memory which my soul will never lay aside. This memory has become a charm against the petty troubles of every day. When I revive it, life and death seem of little account; and the thought of the infinite draws near, as an image mirrored in still waters seems to draw near to one who kneels down upon the bank.

I forgot, that night, that the earth is peopled; and I realised that we humans of this latter day have been inclined to set too much importance upon the peopling of the world. An intimate relationship with nature can in many cases be secured in no other way than by fleeing from human kind and from the conditions of our ordinary life; and thus it comes to pass that that which at the outset was accorded to us as a permanent possession, now seems to us no more than the privilege of an hour. The Satan of our new world compensates us all too richly for the loss of our ancient heritage, and nevertheless at long last we are the losers by the bargain, for the best still eludes us— all which freedom from human entanglements brings with it, the repose of good thoughts, and the peace that comes from a knowledge of one's own self.

IX · · THE REIGN OF THE BEAST · · IX

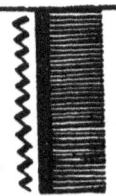HE air induced a feeling of excessive languor. On the second day of our journey to Mangalore, we had entered one of the uppermost extensions of the jungle lying between great rocky slopes.

The descent from the hills and the advance coastwards were slow, for we could march only during the hour before sunrise and two or three hours afterwards. Occasionally we made a short march in the evening; but it was impossible to cover much ground at this time of the day, seeing that the arduous and elaborate preparations for camping occupied the comparatively cool hours before nightfall.

I felt painfully restless, and suffered from a dull sense of oppression which made travelling extremely difficult. It seemed to me as if I could not breathe, as though my blood were bursting its vessels like fermenting wine. I

AN INDIAN JOURNEY

was beset with a giddiness worse than that of drunkenness, and I could not conceive how I had been able to live for months in such a hothouse—for I ignored the fact that the climax of the torrid season had now been reached. Evil memories of my recent attack of fever fell upon me like beasts of prey. I dreaded these memories more than I dreaded the wild beasts that dogged our steps, and even more than I dreaded the venomous serpents whose bite is especially dangerous at this time of year and is apt to prove instantly fatal. To my fancy, the primeval forest was full of this poison, and the exhaustion of the dwellers in the jungle was communicated to my own body, spreading to the chambers of my heart. More than once I imperiously insisted that we must retrace our path to the hills, but Panya and Pasha, hardly troubling to contradict, continued with stoical indifference to follow their own course, which was probably the only right one in the threatening circumstances.

I had become blind to the beauties of the scenery through which we passed. The only thing that sustained me was the thought of the sea. Again and again, despite the deadly peril, and in secret kinship with the suffering lower creation, I besought the heavens for rain. Moreover I had completely lost my place in the map. I knew nothing more than the points of the compass, so that I had to leave myself entirely in the hands of Panya, whose opinions seemed to me the more untrustworthy, the more he tried to buoy me up with false hopes. Frequently we had to change our direction, for we encountered insuperable obstacles, and it was almost impossible to say what progress we were making towards our unknown destination on the coast. Now we were short of food, again of water; and the only thing that saved us from starvation was Panya's knowledge of the multifarious fruits of the forest. Sometimes, despite the spur of hunger, I lacked energy to shoulder my gun. Often enough, my only nutriment for a day was some cocoanut milk, or a pineapple.

From among the privations and distresses of these days there remains to me the memory of an incident to which I owed the last flickering up of my energy. Early one morning, before sunrise, we entered the narrow, rocky outlet of a ravine, which soon expanded to a considerable width. There was still prevailing that strange and thrilling semi-obscurity when the moonlight has not quite vanished before the advance of day. Nowhere but in the tropics have I seen the dawning assume this strange aspect of a struggle for supremacy. In Europe, night seems to flee before day; the stars pale gently, long ere the sun shows itself on the horizon; and the timid moon, which is still sometimes visible in these morning hours, is merely a fading reminiscence of night. But in India, when day dawns, the luminaries of the night encounter his coming with passionate resistance; and the sense of this conflict is impressed all the more deeply because of the stubborn tranquillity with which the stars continue to shine.

It was at this juncture that the voices of the jungle beasts began to greet the coming of day. We were in dense woodland, pushing our way through the undergrowth at considerable distances one from the other, or leaping from rock to rock, across fallen trees, and over marshy pools in which the remnants of a mountain torrent were stagnating. After a while we entered a bamboo grove, and between the stems for a brief space a view could be gained across the huge ravine. On either hand the bare yellow rocks rose almost sheer to the skyline. Farther on they diverged, permitting a glimpse towards the steaming and shimmering grey distance. The jungle looked like a thick, green coverlet lying in the corner of a vast room with golden walls. Above it, the morning sky had the limpidity of glass.

The upper half of the westernmost precipice was tinted red by the light of dawn, whilst on the opposite cliff the green moonlight still flickered. Spellbound by the sight, I stood meditatively watching it. Not only was I filled with the hope that now, perchance, the worst of our journey was over, but I fancied I could detect a cool and refreshing breeze as my gaze lingered entranced on the radiant passage of the sunlight down the wall of the ravine.

About halfway up this wall, just at the level to which the sunlight had descended, a ledge ran along the cliffside, a ledge which might have been taken for the margin of an ancient lake. It produced almost the impression of an artificial roadway, and may, indeed, have been passable for the greater part of its extent, for it ran across vaulted cave-mouths and gave lodgement to isolated dwarf-palms and aloes. In front of the largest of these caverns was a small plateau of rock, no larger than the space which a full-grown lime tree can shade at noon. At the edge of the plateau, something was lying in the sunshine. I can recall that, before I had become fully conscious of the object upon which my eyes were resting, before I had troubled to consider what this tawny, motionless something might be, a subconscious sense of awe had already become dominant in my mind. Then, of a sudden, as if the name had been called to me in a loud voice, and before I had really made out the creature's lineaments, I grew aware of what I was looking at—the tiger.

This was the only time that I saw a tiger in the open. Leaning against the stem of a tree, I closed my eyes, re-opened them, and looked up like one who can hardly trust his sight. Never shall I forget those yellow walls of rock, the morning sunlight streaming into the cave, and in front, as if thrown on a marble pediment and canopied by the cliff, the tranquil sphinx-like figure of the tiger. Owing to the distance, and because he was dwarfed by the rocky surroundings, the beast looked small; but I could distinguish the markings on his coat, and saw the paws on which the terrible head was pillowed—the motionless head which, as if sculptured, completed the graceful line of the back and the mighty neck. His gaze was fixed on the distance. Incomparable was the majesty of this glowing monument of nature.

I was seized with a melancholy whose cause still eludes me, but I know that I clenched my fists and trembled. For the first time I now realised the beauty and the grandeur of the Egyptian sphinx, the most stupendous stone monument which the spirit and the skill of man have ever created. This work of art gives expression to the concepts of God, nature, and mankind, in all their manifold contra-

AN INDIAN JOURNEY

dictions. Most captivatingly does it combine ruthlessness with hope, masterfulness with gentleness, peril with pleasure, and godlike power with sportiveness. Not merely in virtue of the abyss which separates us from this work of sculptured stone, but in its very self and for all times of the past and the future, the sphinx constitutes a titanic monument of history, that history which, in the vast scale of its development, seems to spurn the record of petty details, and is concerned only with measuring by sublime milestones the passage of the millenniums which the human heart traverses in its never-resting pulsation.

The sight of the great cat resting in the sunshine, free on the rocky height, above the uneasy ferment of the manifold lesser animals and plants of the jungle, carried my spirit back across the ages to reach that most ancient of human sculptures. Thus the splendid beast in his solitude loomed before my imagination as if he had been a late survival of vanished days, already overshadowed by imminence of the expulsion of his powerful race from the world of men, the imminence of an extinction he is now doomed to share with many creatures long since forgotten.

Here, however, he was still monarch. His rocky throne sparkled in the rays of the morning sun; and the awakening forest, spreading beneath this royal resting place, trembled at the contemplation of his dignity. Pitiful, weary, and feeble, were the mannikins that were creeping along, sheltered by the undergrowth. I, too, was one of these mannikins, tolerated but apprehensive as they traversed the realm of the beast.

AN INDIAN JOURNEY

In the evening, when I was trying to go to sleep in the tent, I noticed that the sky between the tree stems had a reddish tinge which could not come from the camp fire. Going out, I searched the distance. Moonrise was not due for many hours, but the sky was aglow. I roused Panya.

"The steppes are afire," he said, looking in all directions, and sniffing; but the night was windless, and no smell of burning could be detected. "The hill-sides are blazing," he continued, still heavy with sleep. "The animals are dying by thousands, and among them the noxious beasts. The Malabar hillmen burn off what the sun leaves to burn. Often enough, however, no one knows what starts these fires."

The glow grew more intense; an angry light spread through the forest; the cries of the beasts sounded more isolated than usual, and seemed dulled as if out of respect for the dominant element.

"There is no roar of flames," said Panya, listening. "The fire is creeping quietly over the heights."

He returned to his couch, since we were in no danger. For myself, even before this I had had little hope of sleep, and now I was thoroughly awakened. In imagination I saw the red tongues of flame as they flickered in the blue night over the endless expanse of the hills. I seemed to hear the cries of the beasts in their hasty flight, of the beasts undergoing defeat by man in the unceasing struggle for the possession of the mountains. Towards morning the moon would shine through the smoke, until at length the animated picture would be surmounted by the rocky

AN INDIAN JOURNEY

crests, gold tinted in the rays of the rising sun. In those altitudes peace prevailed; there the everlasting war was not.

From the ravine came the hooting of an owl—sustained notes at distant intervals, now suggesting fear, and now the torment of love. When the sky reddened yet more intensely, the hooting ceased, so that the loneliness of silence was restored to the rocky walls of the ravine where they showed darkly through the ruddy mist; and the night swept on, glowing in its majesty.

The luxuriant vegetation of the forest seemed to exhale a mute unrest. The spirits of a vanished past came to life once more in my memory and began to talk to me. Environing nature seemed morbidly wakeful; from holes, caves, and green crevices peeped the masks of insatiable greed and irritable lassitude; in the bamboo grove the wind slumbered, motionless like a huge butterfly made drunken with poisonous fumes. The uneasiness of the stifling forest had communicated itself to the creatures that dwelt therein, but nought availed: neither cry nor complaint; neither resignation nor angry protest. Only in water or in fire was deliverance to be found. Did not Panya say just now that the undergrowth often ignited spontaneously?

The breathless silence was broken by a dull sound. Was it a cry of bird or beast? No, it was the noise made by a rotting tree as it fell with a sigh into the marshy bed from which it had grown. I listened to the hoarse whispers of decay with which the voices of the dead were guiding my passive thoughts back towards their forgotten realm. The imp of fever again leered at me maliciously with his green

eyes; I felt myself embraced by death and unable to escape from his clutches. With a dull sense of forlornness I realised that I had not yet learned how to die. I ardently desired action, struggle, and effort. I revolted against the demand my surroundings seemed to be making, the demand that I should submissively accept this stagnation of the blood.

Was it because that morning I had looked on the majesty of the lord of the jungle, that I now lacked courage and energy to assert my own right to existence? The afflictions from which nature was suffering, which hour by hour were more urgently and more overwhelmingly communicated to myself, to which indeed I was in danger of succumbing, aroused in me a tormenting conviction of sin. In every tribulation, he who is endowed both with sensitiveness and understanding always tends to seek the fault within his own breast. Those whose minds are awakened, are those that are responsible, those that must make the sacrifice, those that must expiate the sin both in small matters and in great. Had I not shudderingly perceived the tragedy and grandeur of the ancient dominion of force in this land; had I not, as a petty intruder, paid homage after my fashion—though at heart full of sinful pride?

When I closed my eyes, it was as if, across the inert and languishing earth, there had been wafted to me a pestilential vapour from that place into which I had looked where the yellow corpse of the panther was lying in the thicket of bluish-green aloes. Next there flashed into my mind the rock canopy, resplendent in the sunlight, which had overhung the throne of the tiger. To the tiger had

AN INDIAN JOURNEY

been given power over this domain. He was unharmed by the poisonous emanations of the jungle. His tough frame, moved by sinews of steel, luxuriated in the fierceness of the tropical sun. For refreshment, he swam sportively in the raging torrent. Day after day he prowled through the undergrowth, tireless, and with none to challenge his progress.

When an attack of fever is imminent, we suffer from a mingled sense of oppression and dread. At such times the

intelligence is subject to strange fluctuations, in which states of confusion alternate with supernatural clarity of vision. I was now in this condition, and it seemed impossible for me to get far enough away from that boundary at which the transition from the rule of beast over earth to the rule of man occurred. To my alarmed senses it appeared that man was insane in his arrogance; that, trusting to the slender safeguards of his fragile cities, he was absurdly prone to overestimate the extent of his dominion. Once again, meseemed, that the spirit of India and of its

AN INDIAN JOURNEY

ancient peoples visited me and addressed me. I came to grasp the meaning of a doctrine which venerates animals, prays to them, and never slays them; to understand a religious consciousness and a religious faith in which an intimate relationship with the animal creation can be discerned; to appreciate a creed which in its humility esteems passive patience, reverent expectation, and holy quietism. I was reminded of the memorable night of dreams when a monkey had triumphantly related to me his victory over imprisonment.

But just as the vague sentiment of reverence is attended by fear rather than by calm, inasmuch as peace is achieved by the spirit only through knowledge, so did it seem to me in the mysterious perturbations of this hour as if the reign of the beast on earth had not been overcome; but rather did that reign still continue, masked and ostensibly restricted, yet in reality full of its ancient vigour and gloom.

With the weary lineaments of Huc the monkey who had appeared to me at the outset of my thoughtless excursion into the flower-bedecked ruins of this realm of ancient gods, the spirit of those vanished days reappeared to me. Contemplating me with his grey eyes he said:

"The beast still holds sway here, all around you, within the sphere assigned to him by nature. Man has penetrated no farther into nature than a bark-boring beetle into a tree. In man's upright figure, beneath his white skin, behind the sapient forehead and the lovely eyes, nature lies hid. Does not the transformation still take place swiftly and easily beneath his envelope? Not only in battlefields and amid

AN INDIAN JOURNEY

the turmoil of excited crowds, but also in quiet rooms, or in the market-place beneath the martyr's stake, or under the guise of the sweetest-sounding flattery? Still is the beast supreme. The sages of the earth tremble on their path athwart the medley which rages round them, as they hasten forward, sore at heart, with girded loins, upon their earthly pilgrimage."

With fiery tread the night moved sluggishly on its course; the glow from the brushwood burning in the distance faded by degrees, but seemed to have left an increased heat in its train; no cool breath came to herald the dawn. Fruitlessly I scanned the heavens for the morning star. While sullen storm clouds, portentous of evil, gathered in the lurid sky, the voice of my uneasiness monotonously resumed its parable:

"The beast reigns. When morning comes, your blood will have ceased to flow. You will have been suffocated in this sultry, green mantle."

The torment from which I suffered was not aroused by thoughts of bodily death, but by this gloomy realisation of the reign of the beast, and by my utter hopelessness when, on the borderland of madness, I sought an issue, a delivering certainty, a light that should lighten the future. As one who has come to doubt the good faith of his mistress suspiciously studies her life in search of proofs of her infidelity, doing so against his better will, and even against his conscience, so now in these dark hours did my soul study the history of the world in search of marks of the beast, and the sculptured sphinx rose anew before the eyes of my imagination. The vision was merged into old memories

AN INDIAN JOURNEY

of the nature of man, and into my recent reminiscence of the aspect of the recumbent tiger on the rock plateau. This sight, which I had seen but yesterday, seemed, in mystical association with the primeval fears and venerations of our human kind, to have thrown a ray of light into the world of my own consciousness; and that night no sage's wisdom, and no force of conviction could have changed the current of my thoughts.

Among the Egyptians of old there must have been a definite belief that the reign of the beast had not yet been overthrown. They fashioned inseparable organic unities; feline bodies with human heads, and human bodies with leonine heads. Such composite statues were among their deities, and in such forms they recognised themselves.

While my thoughts were still on the look-out for certainty, for a decisive refutation, for a proclamation of the truth that nevertheless the power of the beast was broken, the figure of John approached me, John whom the sage of Golgotha had most dearly loved. He, too, he who more than all others had been transfused with the human grandeur and the divine triumph of his master, was, even in his ecstatic vision of the coming reign of the Son of Man, terrified by the contemplation of the beast. In the Revelation of St. John the Divine, wherein we discern how the affectionate heart of the seer was torn by mingled fears and hopes, we read that the beast appeared to him:

"And I stood upon the sand of the sea, and saw a beast rise up out of the sea, having seven heads and ten horns, and upon his horns ten crowns, and upon his heads the name of blasphemy. . . . And I saw one of his heads as

AN INDIAN JOURNEY

it were wounded to death; and his deadly wound was healed: and all the world wondered after the beast. . . . And they worshipped the beast, saying, Who is like unto the beast? who is able to make war with him? . . . And it was given unto him to make war with the saints, and to overcome them: and power was given him over all kindreds."

The teeming obscurity of the sweltering forest darkened my hyper-vigilant senses, as in the giddiness of an imminent swoon, and my pitiful thoughts flitted to and fro like pallid will-o'-the-wisps. By now the fancy that death was close at hand had become a certainty, and I am confident that never have I been nearer to the valley of the shadow. There still flickered in my heart, a last hope as it were, hardly understood and almost overwhelmed with grief, an intolerable yearning for the morrow. Gasping for breath, I craved for deliverance. Such is the recollection of my ultimate sensations ere I slept, under the menace of the hot breath of the beast.

The dream from which I awakened in the light of morning was sweet and gentle, as if some gracious angel had wished to compensate me for the torment of my night thoughts by instilling a happy confidence. It is often so with us mortals, that the change from despondency to joyousness accompanies the change from sleep to waking, or conversely, as though some purpose were at work to make alleviation attendant upon the natural mutation of our states. Thus can we explain how the events of a happily spent day may be reflected in troubled dreams; or how the

AN INDIAN JOURNEY

faces of the dead, their agony once passed, are apt to suggest a feeling of ineffable peace.

I cannot recall any dream which brought me such serenity; and never have I known a sense of benediction comparable to the repose which came to me in this sleep as a merciful relief from my distressing fears and doubts. Knowledge which is communicated to us in dreams is strangely innocent of experience. It often seems to be free from the errors to which the facile thoughts of the waking brain are prone in their hope to subsume variety under unity and to deduce the particular out of the general. Arduous meditation is the enemy of thought; for good thoughts come to us unawares like light or heat, like a sunbeam piercing the clouds, or like a bud opening beneath the rains of spring. Sleep, therefore, may prove a kindly friend to thought; and the text often quoted in jest, He giveth His beloved sleep, has a no less profound significance than the immemorial desire of man to discover the true interpretation of his dreams.

In a luminous procession, whose sole and sufficient light as it swept forward against a dark background was furnished by one bright pencil of rays from heaven, the saints of history who overcame the beast moved through my dream. Emerging from unfathomable depths lost in uttermost darkness, this train glided onwards in its radiance as if a white brook were flowing in the night across the blackness of earth. At each moment when one of the figures in the procession grew plainly visible, it merged into the great word of its most notable utterance. With the utterance of the word, which poured into my senses like a gleam of light, the countenance and the name of the speaker vanished, and it seemed to me as if this disappearance were in accordance with the sage's own will. In the vague half-light that prevailed close to the moving figures, I could dimly discern that they were accompanied by the formidable shapes of chained beasts. Among them I saw a dragon with a hundred coils; in glowing and splendid though dark tints there loomed and then faded the lion head of Sekmet, above the graceful feminine bust; there, too, came the sacred serpent, crowned, his throat swelling beneath the mouth with its envenomed fangs.

Among the saints there came once more that strangest of all the prophets known to the religions of the nations, whose words concerning the power of the beast I have even now quoted; but on the occasion of this coming his countenance no longer bore traces of the anguish of his martyrdom. He was the last, and with him and his divine word the radiant procession vanished:

"I am . . . the first and the last . . . I am the root and the offspring of David, the bright, the morning star."

X ··· A TYRANT OF THE MARSH ··· X

I CANNOT say how many days elapsed between the night of these intimate spiritual experiences when I encountered the beast, and the morning hour on which Panya's jubilant voice hailed me through the undergrowth. Again and again he had assured me that all would be well, but now for the first time did his loud tones make me fully confident that deliverance was at hand. To begin with I could understand one word only; and since when shouting he was inclined to sing rather than to speak, his full meaning was not clear to me until he stood laughing before me. Then, trembling with delight, he explained that he and Pasha had made their way to the bank of the Kumardhari, the largest river of South Canara. Rising in the hills of Coorg and Mysore, it joins the Netravati at Uppinangadi. Mangalore, our destination, lies at the mouth of the Netravati.

"There is still enough of water in the stream to float a full-sized canoe," said Panya exultantly. "As soon as we have some dug-outs, you will not need to walk another step until you can enjoy the shade of the palm trees in Mangalore. It matters little now when the rains come; the river will bear us swiftly to the sea."

At first I shared his enthusiasm. According to his account we were approaching the right bank of the stream, whose flow here was due south. We must, therefore, have crossed it at an earlier date, presumably during the hot days of happy wanderings before my attack of fever. Soon, a strange sense of disappointment seized me. I felt, it is true, a resurgence of vital energy, and yet this was accompanied by profound depression. Changes were imminent, changes that involved a return to the greyness of ordinary life; and therewith the more intimate realities of my visions grew hazy and unreal. Of course I could never forget the experiences I had just been enjoying, but of a sudden they appeared in some way to have forfeited their ardours. What had seemed so real at the time, would remain as nothing more than a smiling memory. Unquestionably, these lovely happenings of the past had in their day been momentous; but they could no longer be my unique interest, for those of the time that lay before me would now make their pressing claims and would occupy the centre of my attention.

It was then that I made up my mind never to write or speak of my more intimate experiences, but to confine myself to a description of externals. I turned to look backwards, as if my eyes could again have surveyed all the things which had alternately discouraged and rejoiced me. But I could see nothing more than the impenetrable walls of green, with the fan-like palm trees shining in the sun.

AN INDIAN JOURNEY

Our footsteps had left no trace. My passage had been forgotten in the realm through which I had made a brief pilgrimage, which I had but dimly understood, and had loved with a timid affection.

To-day, after the lapse of years, bowed over the white sheets of paper which are to convey my thoughts, my joys, and the images and colours of memory, I am better able to understand the gloom that encompassed my spirit. Then, the hour of the change had just struck. Then, I felt that I ought to cling to the life I was leaving; for there are no associations and no embraces in the world whose joys are comparable to those we derive from a contact with nature. Associations with nature, the embraces of nature, remain innocent and majestic, and are more in accord than any others with the currents of our consciousness. There may moreover have been stirring in my mind secret reminiscences of the haste and the tyranny of European life, a life which cannot bring happiness however busily it may be concerned with human aims and duties. We deafen our spiritual selves by this excess of activity. Happiness is unattainable without the repose of contemplation.

For all that, I was intoxicated at the same time with the prospect of the new things that awaited me; and I already had a premonition as to the nature of the coming experiences. To eager souls, realms of light and storms of the spiritual world herald their coming no less plainly than in the physical domain days of storm or sunshine are wont to forewarn of their advent. For a brief space I felt as if I were seeing through the wilderness of jungle,

AN INDIAN JOURNEY

downwards to the ocean; as if I were watching the bluish smoke of the Indian city floating over the palm trees, some of them stiff and straight like candles, and some leaning to one side. Here and there a white wall was shimmering in the sunlight. The scalloped wooden roof of a temple showed brown above the green tree-crests, and behind it lay the blue expanse of the sea. Such, to my fancy, was the aspect of this dwelling-place of the spirit of eld; and my most intimate longing was to become acquainted with one of the children of this spirit. Occasionally in my journeyings I had encountered Brahmins; but never had I known a Brahmin intimately, for most members of the Brahmin caste who are accessible to strangers to-day have grown indifferent to the Brahmin tradition. Such men are traders; they are no longer priests or sages.

Mangalore, I knew, was a place of great antiquity, almost untouched by the life of the modern world. It was one of the few large towns on the west coast that knew nothing of railways or steamboats. For the most part, only in the remote interior does the regime of the priestly caste persist; but here that regime was still in force in the vicinity of the world's highways. Both the Jesuits and the Protestant missionaries had settlements in the town, so that a strange and lively conflict of spiritual forces was rife in Mangalore.

In such wise was my state of mind unsettled during the last day spent in the forest with my brown-skinned companions. Towards noon we reached a village, lying close to the river on a gentle elevation. Our attention was drawn to it by the trumpeting of an elephant. I had not as yet caught sight of the river, although we were making our way along its marshy bank, but its presence was betrayed by the gurgling and gobbling of waterfowl and by the swampy odour of the air.

After a time we entered a well-trodden and winding path, running like a brown ribbon between high, reed walls. After following this for a considerable distance, we at length encountered a human being, an old woman, nude save for a scanty apron, and carrying a copper pot on a stick over her shoulder. Her eyebrows were stained with henna, and upon her forehead there was painted a dusky caste-mark, resembling a huge spider in form.

When I beckoned to her, she approached timidly. Perhaps I should rather say that she stood her ground and allowed me to approach her. Then, raising her arms, she made a reverence which conveyed her willingness to do any service that might be required, but at the same time it indicated that if the worst came to the worst she was ready to run away.

Panya peeped into the copper pot.

"Ugh!" he exclaimed, "there's a toad in it!"

He and the old woman found it difficult to understand one another. She knew no Hindustani and barely a few words of Canarese; but she was able to explain that the place was called Shamadji; that the king was well disposed towards the white lords; and that he had two elephants, both bulls.

"A fine sort of king he's likely to be," said Panya with an irreverent wink.

AN INDIAN JOURNEY

In Malabar and South Canara there are many of these Hindu kinglets. Towns which were the former seats of their power have long since passed into the hands of the Mohammedans or the British; and the monarchs have withdrawn into the rural districts, where they can live wholly for their people—or rather upon their people. Their kingship has points in common with the genius of many a neglected poet. Cut off from the world, the kingship, like the genius, is apt to develop into a monstrosity, which is impressive only to the eyes of a select company of the faithful. There is something infinitely touching about these despots spiritual or temporal, and he must be a hard-hearted fellow who wishes to rob them of their illusions. So much kindliness is usually to be found behind the mask of vanity, that one should learn to regard vanity without contempt, for that which is truly evil is rarely vain. These wielders of an unrecognised sovereignty are apt to be so greatly moved when a stranger unexpectedly ministers to their sense of self-importance, that their dignity is prone to become formidable as soon as they find it is not contested.

Nevertheless I determined to take the king of Shamadji as seriously as if he had been the Maharaja of Mysore. The trifling presents I might have been able to send him would probably have made very little impression, for in many cases these forgotten rulers are still rich enough to surround themselves with all the gawds that are attainable by way of western commerce. In the first instance, therefore, I despatched Pasha in the old woman's company to ask for an audience, and to say that I craved permission

AN INDIAN JOURNEY

to pitch my tent for a night in the shadow of his throne. Pasha obeyed, with his usual earnestness of demeanour, and without giving any indication as to what he thought of my plans. The old dame twittered with delight, and accompanied him with the most remarkable leaps and bounds which gave token of her vigour but did not enhance her dignity, and certainly must have been unsettling to the toad she had captured.

Panya took exception.

"That is not the way to approach a king, Sahib," he said reflectively. He seemed seriously concerned, and I was expecting him to proceed in quite a different strain, when he continued: "He will clamber upon his mangy old elephant, and will look down upon you as if you were a beggar. But if you had graciously granted him permission to see you, he would have sent you his elephant for your mount, and would have prostrated himself before you when you did him the honour to ride into his palace."

"Understand, Panya, that I do not want the king to see me, but that I want to see the king. I want to see him in his own character, and after the manner in which he habitually lives. Do you think it is pleasanter to look upon a man when he grovels on the ground, or when he encounters one face to face?"

"That is the trouble," answered Panya. "You set no store on your own dignity. If you liked, you could travel through the jungle like a prince; and you prefer to tramp it like a mendicant fakir who has to beg his way. It is a hard fate to have to serve such a master. This king might really have been of some use to us. In the case of other

AN INDIAN JOURNEY

kings, of those who are still wealthy and powerful, your way of approach would have been the only possible one."

Greatly perturbed, he squatted on one of our packages and watched the ants which seemed busily engaged in trying to carry it away. In reality he did not think as he had spoken and could easily have been talked over. His concern was for my prestige and for the figure he was himself likely to cut upon the stage. Since I had no doubt that an opportunity for his play-acting would arrive in due course, I was content to let him sulk awhile.

Suddenly his discontent broke forth anew in speech.

"Please don't imagine that I myself regard you as a pauper or a weakling. I know what you are, Sahib. But what is the use of having a gold-embroidered robe, if the owner wears it inside out? An honourable man shows what he is."

"Panya, it is too hot to argue. Let us rest until the king comes."

"No, no, you must talk the matter out!"

When I made no answer, he fumed, beating a tatoo with his foot on the ground.

"Do you think it's any pleasure to me to know that I am right?" he angrily enquired.

"Nor to me," I answered. "But the gold-embroidered robe is still gold-embroidered."

He shook his head vigorously.

"That does not solve the difficulty, for I am your servant; but you are the master and should therefore always be in the right. Suppose you choose to play the part of the king's servant, but you find yourself troubled because

he is silent and you feel that in truth he is right? You will get up and go. But I can't do that."

"In the realm where I find myself at home, Panya, there is neither master nor servant; there are only living beings, and the goal of all living beings is freedom. But he who genuinely desires freedom does not look to others in search of it; first of all, he directs his gaze within. Thuswise no one need have concern about his rights; everyone has his portion, when everyone knows his own and watches over it."

"If that is what your God teaches you," said Panya, "he does not know the world, and does not know what goes on in it."

"Perhaps he does not know what the world is like, but he knows what it ought to be like."

"Tell me, then, what you mean by freedom? What am I to understand by it?"

"Freedom begins with the insight and the resolve that our actions must no longer be directed with reference to their effect upon others, but upon ourselves. Or, again, we are free when, following the promptings of our own will, we refrain from action. Suppose you strike a man or a beast, which may at times be necessary. Both you and this other creature will feel something. If you are free, it will be indifferent to you what another feels on such an occasion until you have learned to be guided by what you yourself feel. To attend to this matter, and to guide action in accordance therewith, is the first step towards freedom."

"And the last?" enquired Panya.

AN INDIAN JOURNEY

"The last step is the will to transmute all the evil in your heart into love."

"I do not know what is good and what evil. No two people have the same opinions about it. The Brahmins' opinion differs from mine; your opinion differs from that of the fakirs in the hills; and if you enquire of a missionary, his views will make your hair stand on end."

"You are wrong. You know quite well what evil is; and you need know it only for yourself. You have nothing to do with the evil which others have to face. But you know what is evil for you."

"So be it. But suppose I have no love, Sahib?"

"Then you are lost, Panya, for then no god can help you to freedom, neither your god nor mine. Such men are, indeed, poor and wretched."

Panya seemed satisfied with this conclusion of a modest amount of reflection. He smiled as if at the thought that in such case he was not so badly off. But then he began to scratch himself, and, glancing at him in the sunshine, I perceived that he was troubled in his mind. He said cautiously:

"Inside your head, Sahib, your thoughts are not much amiss. But when they come out into the world, and one wants to make practical use of them, it is as if one tried to use sunlight in the darkness of the night. Life is different, that is the trouble."

"It is dark, Panya. But what distinguishes the heart from the hands, is that in the heart the light can be stored up."

Had not a troop of little savages appeared at the bend

of the path to the village, Panya would certainly have excogitated a further objection. For the nonce, however, he could find no rejoinder, seeing that the palpable facts of life imperiously resumed the ascendant. The newcomers were Hindu children, from twenty to thirty in number. Jostling one another in the narrow pathway, some of them were incessantly trying to stand in front of the others, in the endeavour to get a better view. The inevitable result of this manœuvre was that the lively throng drew continually nearer, until at length the strongest boys in the front rank stood their ground sturdily so as not to be pushed any closer to us. Some of them clambered among the pepper vines, and the black eyes and the chubby brown faces were framed by green leaves.

"A message in the head of an old woman is like rice in a coarse sieve," said Panya laughingly.

"There was no young woman there, Panya."

He looked at me with a curious expression of face, and said:

"That is all the same to you, Sahib. You regard the women of my country much as I regard the thoughts of your brain."

I had of late frequently been astonished at Panya's candour, and at his confident tread in the unfamiliar environment of our relationship. This was a delight to me, for the way I treated him would have had unfortunate results in the case of most men of his class and nation.

Panya made a fierce sally towards the living evidence of what appeared to be the chief industry of those who dwelt in this royal city; but he did not produce so great

AN INDIAN JOURNEY

an impression as he had expected. Returning, therefore, he picked up my gun and tried once more. This time the youngsters drew back in alarm. He smiled, well pleased; and delivered an address in Hindustani which must have been all the more impressive to them because they could not understand a word of it. His harangue was interrupted by a distant fluting and the clash of cymbals, whereupon he promptly came back to me.

"There is the king!" he said. "He would have kept you waiting longer but for his curiosity."

The noisy music drew nearer, arousing expectant thoughts as to what was approaching behind the green curtain of undergrowth. Its rhythm was strangely exciting. The first thing to come in view was the grey head of an elephant, surmounted by a brightly coloured cotton canopy, somewhat crookedly supported by four staves, three of which were gilded whilst one was of simple iron. In the howdah was a deck-chair made of cane, and on this sat the king of Shamadji turning his head eagerly in all directions on the look-out for the visitor to his kingdom. Eight retainers, disposed on either side of the elephant, carried fans made of peacock's feathers attached to thin bamboo rods. These fans were a trifle the worse for wear, their rainbow eyes were to some extent blinded; and the attire of the train suggested the haste of impromptu preparations. Nevertheless the procession was by no means lacking in splendour. Above all, the elephant's trappings were extremely handsome, being made of beautiful stuffs, richly embroidered, and decked with imitation jewels the size of a man's fist. The musicians, contrary

AN INDIAN JOURNEY

to the usual custom, marched behind the elephant. Presumably the king had been unwilling to allow them the front places. The consequence was that their aspect was not so much one of solemnity as of curiosity, for they were doing their utmost to catch sight of the stranger by peering to the right and left of the king's unwieldy mount. Behind them, in disorderly array, was the entire population of the village.

We made our way to a clearing, and the king bowed to me ceremoniously, after quieting the music with a wave of his brown hand. Having glanced searchingly at my baggage, he bade me welcome in the English tongue. I answered in the same language. Panya interpreted, for he did not believe that the king's English would go very far, and he was right in his supposition.

Now the monarch nimbly alighted from the back of his elephant, treading as unconcernedly on the shoulders of his retainers as if they had been a wooden stepladder. He kept his distance, as a hint that he had no taste for a western handshake, while I passed a few compliments concerning his power and prestige, with which, I said, the jungle was resonant. These remarks were greatly to his taste, and he went on to inform me that he possessed another elephant which, however, he had not brought along to-day. His city was open to me, and I was welcome to pitch my tent in his palace garden. We were standing in a brown and white ring of gaping onlookers, in the shade of the elephant. After we had exchanged some additional courtesies, the king asked what he could do for me.

Panya hastily advised me to say that I was on a govern-

AN INDIAN JOURNEY

ment mission, but I could not bring myself to do this, so I answered that I had come to visit his country and his capital, of which I had heard in the west. I do not think that Panya translated this accurately, but whatever he said, it did not put me out of favour with the king, who accompanied us to the village—always keeping his distance, and displaying extreme rudeness towards his own people.

"Are you an Englishman?" enquired the king, and Panya answered before I could put in a word:

"The Sahib would like to know whether you are a king!"

It was a home thrust. I was amazed at the placid way in which the affront was swallowed. Those only who have witnessed the cool self-assurance of the British officials in the interior of India, will understand that the counter-question which Panya had put into my mouth was quite within the limits of customary British arrogance. I was to pass myself off as an Englishman! The announcement of my German nationality would probably have produced about as much impression upon this prince as would be produced in Berlin by a negro who should proudly announce himself of Ashanti stock.

We crossed the village square, which was surrounded by mangroves, looking like huge greyish-green tents. Their interlacing aërial roots, like the lattice-work of a cage, made it difficult to see the huts, which were almost hidden by the foliage. The palace was at the farther end of the village, in a grove of wild lemon trees and areca palms. It was a two-storied building of white plaster, and was surrounded by a tall cactus hedge, between the stems of which were termite heaps forming natural turrets. The windows were shaded with bamboo sunblinds, and were mysteriously silent in the afternoon light falling obliquely athwart the palms; but from time to time the rods of these hangings clicked, as if gently pushed by the hand of an inquisitive inmate.

I was admitted only to the courtyard of the house. After our first brief interview, I should probably have seen nothing more of the king, had it not been for an exciting incident which riveted my interest, and, though I was not in search of adventure, involved me in perilous complications.

When the night had swiftly fallen, and we were sitting in front of the tent after finishing our supper, I heard from the darkness of the garden a plaintive chanting, strangely poignant in its forlornness. The sound recalled the chanting of those who are working in solitude, believing that no one is watching them or listening to them. The notes were sustained and monotonous; they recalled the moaning of an animal. It recurred again and again, luring me with an elemental fascination, so that I felt impelled against my will to make search for its source. Panya insisted on accompanying me in my expedition through the dark garden. The stars were shining brightly. On either side of the narrow path, the huge leaves of the banana trees looked like the ruinous columns of a pagan rampart against the power of malignant gods, or hung tattered in the starlight like the hide of some lacerated monster.

"The king will provide us with boats," said Panya in low tones, "but he wants us to pay him on a scale befitting his dignity. He has chosen oarsmen, and will even supply bananas, papaws, and seasoning for our rice."

I nodded in silence. We said nothing concerning the lamentations which had lured us forth. Maybe Panya assumed that I knew what I was about. Perhaps a certain sense of awe restrained him from talking, just as it restrained me from asking questions.

Close to the cactus hedge we saw after a time the wooden pagoda of a temple, large and black against the sky. The garden afforded a view into the courtyard of this temple, and we could make out the sacred goat among the brown pillars on the threshold of the sanctuary. Nothing stirred. A faint, reddish light glowed from behind a curtained doorway. The interior was hidden from our gaze by hangings of pale red silk.

As we approached a bamboo grove, behind the feathery outlines of which a squat building was visible, the melancholy chanting ceased, just as the noise of the cicadas ceases in the tall grass when a nocturnal wanderer approaches. We pushed on between the tall stems, along a narrow and barely perceptible track. Above us the stars shone through a lattice-work of bamboo leaves and looked like tiny lanterns. In the blackness, behind a grated door, could be heard a faint groaning, which seemed to come from somewhere close to the wooden staves.

"We must have a light," I said to Panya softly.

But this would only have been possible by the use of a torch that would have betrayed us. Assuredly our royal host would have been ill-pleased to find us spying on his household by night.

AN INDIAN JOURNEY

"Wait but a while, and our eyes will get used to the darkness," said Panya.

As I stood irresolute, I could hear my heart beating.

"Is it an animal?" I asked Panya.

He looked at me in amazement at my guilelessness.

"An animal? No, it is a woman," he returned. "Perhaps love has wounded her; perhaps she is being punished."

A fetid, stifling vapour made me gasp when I pressed closer to the wooden grating. The effect of Panya's words on me had been to change alarm into the unthinking courage of anger. I drew to one side, so that the starlight might shine into the dark aperture. The tiny house had solid walls and was like a neglected stable.

"Who is there?" I enquired in Canarese.

Panya stood close behind me. After a brief period of troubled waiting, I perceived a small human face, sickly in its pallor, which now showed itself at the grating. The face was framed in loose strands of black hair, and on either side by terribly lean fingers, grasping the staves of the grating on a level with the eyes. In the dark, this apparition was horrible in its suggestion of doom, as if the face we saw were that of one who had long since died and had now risen from the tomb. The large, dark eyes drank in the night, and shadowed it forth once more in paralysing tranquillity. I felt as if my heart had stopped beating. I staggered, and grasped Panya's arm.

"Come away, Sahib," said he. "If she is ill, the pestilence may seize you likewise."

"Is she ill?"

"I don't know," he answered dubiously.

AN INDIAN JOURNEY

"You know perfectly well," I cried, clenching my teeth. Panya took alarm.

"All I know, Sahib, is that unfaithful wives are punished in such a fashion in this country. But she may be ill."

Beside myself with indignation, I seized the grating with both hands, set my feet against the threshold, and endeavoured, with all the strength which intense anger will sometimes lend us, to break down the barrier. But it was made of strong bamboo and unbreakable.

Panya drew me away from the grating. I could not recall that he had ever ventured to touch me before. His boldness did more than anything else to sober me. When I thought the matter over I realised that the position was a very difficult one, though I was firmly resolved to do my utmost to help this unfortunate being. After all, the affair had nothing to do with me. The king would never forgive my meddling with his private affairs. It was true that he was not so formidable a potentate as he imagined, or as he gave himself out to be; but, conversely, my own status was less secure than he supposed. It is a part of British policy in India to leave the utmost latitude to the wealthier Hindus, and also to the Brahmins, in all concerns of their domestic life. The white rulers have learned that the existence of caste divisions and divergent customs makes it easier to govern the country. Few as they are in numbers when compared with the natives, they form a united and compact society which is more potent than the most powerful of the castes.

I bethought myself that I could look for no protection

AN INDIAN JOURNEY

from a government by whose canons such action as I designed would be most emphatically condemned—all the more if the aggressor were a German.

Nevertheless I was determined to carry out my design, and I decided to send Panya to the king early in the morning, to request an audience. It is remarkable how much easier we find it to do cruel or unjust actions than to tolerate them when done by others. Throughout a sleepless night, spent in the oppressive heat under a mosquito net, the thought of the miseries of this imprisoned woman inspired me with intense wrath against her tormentor. During brief lapses into an uneasy half-sleep, the waxen brown face of the captive appeared before me in a burning mist, and the plaintive chanting of the feeble voice filled the night air, pregnant with disaster and approaching storm.

I arose at the first glimmer of dawn, filled with a desire that had now become painful in its intensity to set eyes once more upon the sea, to gain distant outlooks, to glimpse the image of freedom. It was as if the green walls had dulled my eyes and my senses; I felt inexpressibly irritable, and as if on the verge of suffocation. When one is in such a state, an idea obstinately held may gain added force. There can be no doubt that my mood served to accentuate the wrath in which ere long I went to interview the king. Little I recked the hazards of my conduct. Perhaps that accounts for my success, where cautious approach might have failed.

"You are keeping a woman prisoner in your garden," I said roughly. "It is unworthy of a great prince to treat a helpless creature thus. I demand that you should set her free, instantly!"

For a moment the Hindu sovereign was nonplussed. Then he assumed a supple manner, simultaneously obstinate and deferential, while continuing to display a ceremoniousness which would have wearied the patience of a saint. Panya was extremely serious, and translated everything literally. I felt that on the present occasion he shrank from taking any responsibility.

"I see that you are unwilling to comply with my request," I said, "so I must remind you of the law of the government which forbids murder and punishes it with death."

The king turned pale, and his lips trembled; but his manner remained friendly, and he endeavoured to convince me that he had inflicted no more than a trifling punishment which was well within his rights. Besides, I was interceding without knowing anything of the woman's offence. He was aware that the British were severe, but never yet had he had reason to doubt their justice. He would more readily believe that an unjust man was not an Englishman, than that an Englishman could commit an injustice. Once more did I grasp the cunning and tenacity of these people; once again did I realise the crafty manner in which they can make a weapon of the most trifling doubt, without ostensibly giving offence. Strictly speaking it behoved me to give way, pending an examination into the rights of the matter, or until I had heard why the punishment had been inflicted. But the fact that I had been driven into a corner made me angry instead of circumspect, and I therefore retorted in anger:

"If the British had learned their justice from Indian princes, you would find yourself behind that grating before I had made my way back to Bombay."

It is not my usual practice to treat kings so rudely, but after my opening moves, this was the only possible course. I have no love for the prudence of those who would pitch their tents upon a battlefield from which a generous scheme has been routed by cowardice. I saw in Panya's face that he thought my rejoinder a good one. He now stepped forwards and said quietly:

"The prisoner's legs from the knees downwards have been gnawed by the ants."

The king made Panya no answer. He looked straight in front of him, as if the affair had suddenly ceased to interest him, and at my opponent's change of manner fear for the first time stole into my heart. I felt that he was meditating the use of force, against which spiritual weapons are of no avail. His was an image of the outward dispassionateness in which evil, at bay, meditates perfidy.

"I will set the prisoner free, Sahib Collector," he said quietly.

Unquestionably this title was not used in good faith, for a collector in India is the chief government official of a district, and such a magnate would not have been travelling with an equipment like mine through the remote jungles of Canara. Of course I knew this, and the king's lowering expression was not needed to convince me of the malevolent nature of his onslaught.

AN INDIAN JOURNEY

"Had the Collector been of mind to come, I should not have come myself," I answered brazenly.

All I cared about now was to find suitable repartee. I looked my challenge at the king with tranquil eyes, and I am sure that their colour was more disturbing to him than my presumption. He glanced at me once more, with a look of suppressed malice. In his weary eyes there gleamed the dark poison of the jungle night, hatred of the foreigner, and the racial animosity of an oppressed nationality.

I deemed it prudent to be satisfied with the concession, and to await the issue. I therefore took leave of the king, and at our parting we outvied one another in ceremonious politeness. I had the tent struck and made all preparations for departure, but was fixed in my resolve not to embark until I had learned of the event. I hardly had time to wonder whether success or failure would prove more embarrassing, for, ere the last box had been packed, two of the king's retainers brought the prisoner. The young woman wore a white saree. She walked slowly and with difficulty. When she stood before me, little more than her eyes were visible, and the look of terror in them utterly disconcerted me.

Panya began to talk to her, and with great difficulty was at length able to make her understand that she owed her liberation to us, and that she was free to go wherever she pleased.

She sank to the ground in her exhaustion, continually closing her eyes, which were unused to the light. She showed neither gratitude nor joy. At length, when I had moved away, she asked Panya whether she must accompany the white lord.

Panya told her that we neither demanded nor expected anything of her. He described the allurements of freedom with all the eloquence at his command. After a little time he came to me, and, without either triumph or partiality, but obviously baffled, said:

"Sahib, the young woman begs that you will allow her to return."

"Return to prison?"

"Yes, Sahib. She laid her hands on her heart and named the name of the king."

An hour later our boats shoved off from the landing stage of Shamadji into the sluggish current of the Kumardhari, which quietly bore us westward towards the sea.

Love tolerates no outside interference; it is more independent and more enduring than any other human sentiment; its assurance does not spring from reason, but from a higher inspiration.

XI • • • • • MANGALORE • • • • • XI

THE mere fact of our conscious existence has always seemed to me most wonderful at the moment of waking. When our senses are awakened by the light of the morning sun or by the song of a bird, when consciousness is renewed, the heart is sometimes flooded with a thrill of happiness and astonishment at the certainty of being alive, at the conviction that for countless days which have passed we have moved, and that for countless days which are yet to come we shall move, full of life and vigour, across the sunlit world. Never have I been more keenly aware of this joyous wonder, than upon the morning when I wakened in the boat upon the Netravati river. On the previous evening we had found a backwater, still as any lake, its surface covered with a green luxuriance of strange marsh vegetation. Since it was impossible to get the boat to the land across this tangle, Panya suggested that we should spend the night on the water. I never noticed in the morning when the boat in which I was sleeping was pushed back into the current; and I did not awaken until the sun was up, when the ripple of the water began to arrest my attention. By degrees only did I recall my situ-

[196]

ation, and indeed the sense of time seemed to lapse altogether for a space. In a rush of consciousness free from the limitations of time, I was aware only that the sun was shining on the earth, that birds were calling from the trees, and that I myself was alive.

In subsequent meditation, such moments often gain in significance; as time passes, their magnitude seems enhanced, for memory stores our experiences, not in accordance with their duration and their intrinsic value, but their impressiveness. The manifest significance of an experience is not what determines its preservation in memory. As a rule we are apt to find that trifles are remembered with extraordinary persistence, so that we smile at this, without realising that their energies are derived from a moral realm peculiar to themselves, and one whose mystical essence is entirely independent of the will. "When God's eyes, which are continually sweeping over the regions of creation, light upon our existence, the moment is forever preserved in our memory." These were the words of a Buddhist monk from Cashmir, who was wandering through Malabar in search of a holy tree with grey flowers. Thus it comes to pass that moments we have imagined to be of supreme importance would often sink into oblivion were it not that the memory of them is sustained by the recollection of seemingly trifling incidents.

I sat up in the boat and watched the banks slipping past. So thickly were they overgrown, that it appeared as if we were flying noiselessly and swiftly between crumbling green walls, along a lane that opened out from time to time, and then narrowed once more. This passage-way was roofed by the blue sky, almost unreal in its sparkling majesty of colour; and from time to time, at turns in the stream, the blinding rays of the morning sun forced me to close my eyes.

The previous day had been an arduous one. We had passed Uppinangadi without visiting the town, and making only so long a midday halt as was necessary to give the oarsmen a rest. In the first stages of our voyage they had had more steering to do than rowing. They stood to their work, shifting the oars from side to side of the canoe as the exigencies of the current demanded. To watch their skill entertained me for a long time. While we were on the Kumardhari, the boats would occasionally ground on a sandbank, and on these occasions we all had to stand in the water in order to float our craft once more. At times we circled in whirling pools, and at times had to navigate rapids. I had to get used to the rapids, for at first it was an alarming experience to shoot them, mindful of the possibility that the boat would capsize, and that its crew would be washed by the troubled water to the marshy bank, to be seized there by the alligators, or drowned in the rapids or the whirlpools.

Supremely beautiful was it at night. Generally speaking, we did not travel after dark. But the night before we passed Uppinangadi we continued our course down stream. The moving torches on the banks, looking like gigantic fireflies, were strangely stimulating to the imagination, and reminded us that we were approaching populous regions.

Farther down the Netravati, the river became more sluggish, and we were now dependent on the oarsmen for our progress. In the winding stream, the two boats were often out of sight of one another for a considerable time. There was, however, no occasion for anxiety, for Pasha, who was in charge of the baggage in the second boat, was respected by the men from Shamadji, as persons are apt to be respected when they are habitually silent, and, without being rude, never respond to a smile and rarely answer a question. The porters had been paid off in Shamadji. After a three days' voyage we reached Mangalore, and the canoes instantly started on the return journey. The oarsmen did not set foot ashore. The Shamadji folk are not on the best of terms with the coast dwellers, whom they regard as renegades and as too receptive of foreign ways.

For the last few hours we had been moving slowly through turbid, motionless water. The vegetation here was less luxuriant. Rice-fields alternated with marshy solitudes. They were overhung by heavy vapours, and abandoned by man and beast. It was there that the plague slept through the hot season, to reawaken when the rains set in. The heat was so oppressive that breathing was a painful exertion. Towards the end, the rowers worked almost in a trance. From time to time they rested silently on their oars. The river had broken up into numerous channels. Over the tops of the palm trees I could see the red chimney of the German tile-workers.

We rowed through the town to the harbour, a desolate place, cut off from the sea by a sandbank. The sea air seemed utterly stagnant, and was a bitter disappointment to me. We had seen hardly anything of the town, which lies on three slight elevations, and is hidden in palm groves. Here in the harbour, however, the houses were visible. They were mean in appearance, inhospitable looking, built of badly weathered stone, and exhibiting the roughness and utter lack of character peculiar to certain oriental seaports which have lost touch with their ancient traditions and whose new customs and institutions are subservient to the spirit of unashamed and predatory commercial enterprise. A few antiquated sailing boats with high prows and wide decks were lying untidily, half in the water and half sunken in the mud. No human beings were visible, except for one Hindu, squatting in the shade on a steam launch, and smoking. He looked at us inquisitively. When I rose in the boat, he sprang to his feet and shouted a word or two towards the dirty windows of a painted house. His little vessel served the needs of passenger traffic between the coast and the ocean-going steamers. These have to anchor several miles out at sea, and to wait two or three hours for their passengers. Vessels drawing much water cannot enter the port of Mangalore.

My first impressions of Mangalore were all the more unfavourable because of the life I had been leading for so long, and because of my inclination to compare what I now saw with the splendid simplicity of untouched nature.

Moreover, the town seemed asleep, so that my general impression was one of sloth, decay, and listlessness. The ramshackle Hindu hotel in which I had to spend the first few days was not calculated to revive my energies; and the weary waiting for the breaking of the monsoon deprived

AN INDIAN JOURNEY

me, as it deprived everyone, of the joy of life. A few months later, when Mangalore was burgeoning in the fresh, spring sunshine, the place was almost unrecognisable. In Germany, the differences between summer and winter have far less effect upon the behaviour and feelings of men than have the changes of season in the tropics. The notion that tropical climates are equable, and that in these regions eternal summer prevails, is the outcome of ignorance, or of the fallacious reports of casual tourists. One who has lived the year round close to the equator, one who has watched the tropical population through the joys and sorrows of the changing year, will find the diversities of the seasons in the temperate zone comparatively insignificant.

Subsequently in Mangalore I learned to understand a great deal which at first I had regarded with contempt; I learned to love much which at the outset had seemed strange and repellent; and when I left the town I was inspired with the conviction that no inhabited spot in the world can compare with Mangalore at once for its blissful splendour and its mouldering decay. In our brief, mortal span we never gain sufficient experience of new places and conditions to be able to form just valuations at first sight.

I was in an intensely irritable condition when on the third day after I reached Mangalore I made up my mind to call on the Collector, to enquire about the possibility of my making a long stay, and to ask for information as to the dwellings that were available, and as to the general conditions of life.

AN INDIAN JOURNEY

All the natives I had approached concerning these matters had shown an incomprehensible unwillingness to return straight answers. Some of them were afraid of getting into the bad graces of the government; some feared the priests. Offers of money seemed to appeal only to the scum. The official's bungalow was beautifully situated on a shady hill-side, and reminded me of an old country seat. The garden was in beautiful order; the office I entered was clean, cool, and spacious. In the ante-room, a Eurasian, in white, semi-European attire, was seated at a large writing-table, with an air of being extremely busy. At first I was as unassuming as my irritable nerves would allow, but this underling's impudent pretensions of intimacy with a civilisation which was beyond his comprehension made me lose my temper. I am sure I should have been able to maintain my self-command had not Panya been with me.

"Stand up when I speak to you," I said.

My blood boiled. At this season of the year, when the blood is already so near the boiling point, a very trifling annoyance is sufficient to make the pot brim over.

The clerk slowly rose to his feet, moving as if his limbs were weighted with lead, but his look of impudent amazement inflamed my wrath, and before he was fully erect upon his lean brown shanks, the highly respectable room echoed to a sound of a box on the ear which was as gratifying to me as a douche of cold water. To him, it was probably less agreeable. He spun round, and his office chair obediently followed the movement. Paling on the unsmitten cheek, he struggled for composure. The darker half of his ancestry counselled him to make for the street.

"I wish to see the Collector," I said genially.

I felt enormously better, but it was long ere I was able to understand the cause of my roughness. No doubt my thoughtless outburst and my lack of self-control were dependent on the fact that I had spent nearly six months among persons who had never dreamed of claiming equality with me, so that the manifest self-assertion of this Eurasian seemed far more presumptuous than the offender had designed.

The poor fellow, who had been terribly aggrieved alike spiritually and physically, made it his first concern to battle for his affronted official dignity—after he had placed a distance of about twelve feet, and a worm-eaten table, between himself and me. He was bursting with indignation. Even his oiled hair, shining conspicuously now that he had lost his grey linen cap in the encounter, seemed to radiate protest.

To be ready for all eventualities, I took up from the table an ebony box, containing steel nibs, an ink eraser, and some small copper coins, arranged with the care that might have been given to a queen's jewels. At the first disrespectful word, I was determined to throw it at his head! I have heard that peasants, when their crops are threatened by a hailstorm in excessively hot weather, fire cannon at the clouds in the hope that these may break up in rain. I must have been animated by a similar hope and a kindred belief. But it came neither to an exchange of high words nor to an exchange of blows between me and

AN INDIAN JOURNEY

my adversary, for the inner door now opened, and the Collector, with a calm expression on his clean-shaven face, appeared upon the scene. His gaze wandered from me to his subordinate, and back to me once more.

Our respective attitudes, the table between us, the way in which the clerk was holding a hand to his cheek, and my own pugnacious attitude, must have sufficed to acquaint the ruler of South Canara with what had just taken place. Englishmen of culture occupying prominent posts in the Indian Civil Service display remarkable presence of mind in emergencies. They understand perfectly how to take things as they are, without being in too great a hurry to indicate how they think things ought to be. The Collector turned to me with a polite enquiry whether his intervention might not aid in the restoration of harmony. Thereupon, he motioned me towards the open door of his room, and I entered without lodging any complaint, for it was obvious that he did not wish me to do this in the presence of an underling. Speedily, therefore, I found myself seated in a comfortable wicker chair, facing a man of fifty or more, strong and well set-up, with a shrewd and kindly face which instantly inspired me with confidence. Since he was my senior by thirty years or so, it was easy for me to beg that he would not regard my unceremonious conduct as any sign of disrespect for the British government or his own person. When I mentioned my name, he quietly told me his, and asked whether I was an Englishman.

How important this little matter seems to the British! At my answer, a slight shadow of displeasure flitted across his face, and he enquired whether I belonged to the German mission in Mangalore.

"You infer that I do, from the way I treated your clerk?"

He smiled and shook his head. Taking my question as sufficient answer to his own, he waited for me to proceed. While I spoke he unostentatiously watched me, without manifesting any sign of criticism. For all his features showed, my person and my words might have been offensive to him, or agreeable, or indifferent. When I paused for a moment, he rang a bell on his table and gave an order to the servant who entered. Promptly and silently, this man reappeared bearing a tray with whiskey, soda-water—and ice.

My heart went out to my host with an affection as great as I could have felt for a father; and the feeling was enhanced when, quite simply, the Collector warned me that I had better be cautious in the way I slaked my thirst, for no doubt I had not been used to ice with my liquor in Shamadji. He had been interested in the recital of my adventure with the king. After a time he said:

"A good many years ago, during the first hot season I spent in India, I felt like a murderer; in the second I gave myself up to despair; and not until the third did I begin to feel like an Englishman once more. You need not worry because you have let yourself get out of hand for a moment or two. In India people begin by losing their patience, and then often enough they lose their reason. It is only the exceptions who recover both, but those who do so have learned how to use them."

AN INDIAN JOURNEY

This remark recalled me to the purpose of my call, and the information I wanted was speedily forthcoming. It was on a later visit to the Collector that I first heard the name of Mangeshe Rao, the Brahmin. At the mere sound of his name, and as I listened to a brief and not markedly sympathetic story of his life, I felt drawn to him by a feeling which far transcended curiosity or interest. It was in connection with my request for the name of a cultured Brahmin in Mangalore with whom I could advantageously associate, that the Collector told me the following story, at a time when I had become fairly intimate with this British official.

"Mangeshe Rao is one of the most notable and certainly one of the ablest among the younger Brahmins of Mangalore, and, indeed, of all South Canara. I am not in a position to give you any information as to his real character, for the only relations between such as he and myself are of a political kind, and the stress of public dissensions is peculiarly apt to veil the characters of those with whom, politically speaking, we are at odds. This man has given us a good deal of trouble, and he would have been positively dangerous had he been able to arouse the full sympathy of other members of his caste, and to secure their unanimous support. He was at Madras University, and is therefore thoroughly well educated, in so far as the British universities of India are competent to secure such a result. For this very reason he has forfeited the confidence of the Brahmin caste, whereas for a long time he enjoyed the confidence of the British officials—though I myself have always had my doubts of the man. It was my duty as a civil servant to help him in his efforts in so far as he seemed likely to be useful to us. But always when he was sitting opposite me in that very chair, I was troubled by a feeling of secret alarm at his inscrutability. He soon secured an important post at the English College here; he associated with the Jesuits; he was present at secret meetings of his fellow countrymen; he even hobnobbed with the Protestant missionaries. A friendly feeling was shown him wherever he went. I could never make up my mind whether it was genuine, or was merely inspired by dread.

"Six months ago he lost his post at the College. I have not thought it wise to take any further steps against him, for I know that his influence is extensive, and that he has a wide circle of supporters, not so much in this province as in other parts of India. We have to be careful to avoid inflicting any punishments which may suggest that we are inspired with revengeful feelings. We must only take such measures as are likely to reduce an opponent's influence. This is the sort of thing we're up against. One of the Jesuit fathers in Mangalore called on me a while back, bringing me a small school-book, written in Malayalam, and of the kind, as far as general appearance and get-up are concerned, used everywhere in government schools and mission schools. Let me show it you."

Rising, he went to his safe, and, after a little search among documents, unearthed a grey book, like one of our western copybooks, and handed it to me. It was simple and businesslike in appearance. Like any other text book it had a title-page, bearing the name of the book, and beneath, the imprint of the Jesuit printing house in Mangalore. This is maintained by the mission for its own purposes, and can print in at least ten of the native scripts. The Collector translated the title for my benefit.

"A Text Book of Comparative Philology, showing the Relationship between the Dialects of Southern India and Sanscrit. By Mangeshe Rao, teacher at the English College in Mangalore. Printed by the S. J., Mangalore."

The first ten pages of this modest little work bore out the legend on the title-page. The rest of the book, however, was an able and searching criticism of the British government in the southern provinces. Composed for propagandist purposes, it was all the more effective because it was circumstantial in character and showed a thorough knowledge of the subject, without saying anything that could be accounted positively treasonable. At a later date I got Panya to translate it for me.

The Collector continued: "The Father told me that this misuse of the printing works had been discovered by accident. He felt that by informing me of what had happened he had discharged his society's responsibility towards the government; and he told me that the printers who had been bribed to do this piece of work had been dismissed. I asked him to tell me whom he suspected to have been the author of the pamphlet. He answered civilly that he and his colleagues certainly had their suspicions, but that it was contrary to the views and practice of his order to charge anyone with an offence upon mere suspicion. Manifestly, the mission was afraid, as everyone is afraid here except those who belong to the unthinking crowd. Too often has it happened that some zealous party leader has been found poisoned some fine morning, poisoned by his political enemies. Of course it was my business not to show the white feather, but in India boldness that is not guided by caution isn't worth a row of pins. Before I had taken proceedings, it became plain to me that a rash onslaught would bring me into conflict, not with some casual criminal, but with a powerful organisation having affiliations throughout Hindustan. The matter was beyond my competence. I passed the responsibility on to headquarters.

"I need hardly say that active measures were requisite. Caution did not mean that there was nothing to be done. I asked Mangeshe Rao to call on me. I shall never forget the meeting. At first the Brahmin sent me a message to say it would be more convenient to him to call at some later date. I was amazed, for I was naturally led to suppose, either that he had absolutely nothing to do with the affair or that he was contemplating flight. I therefore had him watched unobtrusively. I now know that he had designed to force me to set spies on him, in order that he might learn whether the matter was serious. He knew at once when he was put under supervision, and came to see me the very next day.

"In the course of a conversation on indifferent matters, I suddenly handed him the book.

"Taking it, and glancing at it, he said politely:

" 'I will examine it as soon as I can find time.'

" 'You are the author,' I said.

" 'Yes,' he answered with calm irrelevance, as if I had

said something quite different, 'I think that will happen soon.'

" 'The book has your name on the title-page as author,' I resumed; and I must confess I was both puzzled and annoyed.

"Mangeshe Rao kept his eyes fixed on me as if expecting me to continue speaking of the nominal topic of our conversation, which had nothing whatever to do with the book. He continued to hold this, absent-mindedly. At length, following the direction of my gaze, and seeming now for the first time fully aware of what I was looking at, he began to flutter the pages—not, as anyone else in his position would surely have done, confining his attention to the innocent opening, but plunging straightway into the attack on the government.

"Glancing up for a moment, with brows a trifle puckered, he courteously said: 'Excuse me,' and went on reading. After a time he turned back to the cover, re-read the title, smiled whimsically, and went on reading. He sat there for a quarter of an hour, under my very eyes, reading his own text, displaying neither astonishment nor anger, showing no emotion of any kind. Indeed, throughout the whole interview, I, rather than he, must have appeared to be the person under examination. I kept my composure, and realised all the time that he was imperturbably cogitating why I was so forbearing. A little later, however, when he shook his head, and smilingly began to read aloud a peculiarly apt and malicious passage, looking up at me to mark the emphasis, I needed the utmost self-command to answer smile with smile. Then he thoughtfully put down the booklet, and with an air of surprise and concern, said:

" 'This is very unpleasant for us.'

" 'Have you any idea who the author can be?'

"As Mangeshe Rao made no answer, I had to ask another question.

" 'How do you suppose your name came to be used?'

"The Brahmin now answered my previous question, after scanning my face for a moment with an expression that seemed to hint his opinion that number two had been a trifle crude.

" 'I have no idea who the author can be. But what surprises me more than anything else is how the Jesuits can have been so heedless as to allow their printing plant to be used by persons who are attacking the very government which protects the Jesuit mission.'

"It seemed as if there were only these alternatives: either frankly to declare my suspicions of the Brahmin; or else to close the interview. I could not do the former without producing my proofs; and I did not wish to do the latter. I therefore again chose a middle course, though I felt it would be futile.

" 'I wonder how the author came to select your name,' I said out loud, but as if speaking to myself.

"Mangeshe Rao's opinion was, after the fleeting glance he had had at the booklet, and taking an impartial view of the level of culture which found expression in the work, that this misuse of his name could hardly be supposed to compromise him. In a more serious vein he continued:

" 'The device of using my name was obvious. If the

book were to be printed in Mangalore, the best mask would naturally be the name of one of the teachers at the English College. But perhaps the chief reason was the need for fooling the Jesuits.'

" 'An English name would have served just as well.'

"Consulting the title-page once more, and then inclining his head modestly, Mangeshe Rao remarked:

" 'That would hardly have done; for in India, everyone who can read knows what poor linguists the British are.'

"I swallowed the affront, realising that I had taken a false step. But my adversary's master-stroke of diplomacy was his leave-taking, in which he refrained from showing the least indication of triumph. He went away sedately and even exhibited a little concern, as if he were gradually beginning to realise that this strange disclosure might prove more inconvenient for him than he had at first imagined. At that very time I held the proofs which I subsequently sent to headquarters. There can be no doubt whatever that Mangeshe Rao was the author of the pamphlet. Later, indeed, he scornfully admitted it in words whose full meaning could be obvious to me alone. His removal from his post at the College was effected by arrangement. The government gave polite assurances that no suspicion attached to him personally, but added that since his name had been used in the affair it was desirable that he should be relieved of his functions for a time."

Such was the history, compiled from numerous details, which came to my knowledge by degrees, of Mangeshe Rao, the Brahmin. Naturally my expectations had been

keenly aroused when, a few weeks later, the day came on which I was to make his acquaintance.

Meanwhile the rains had begun.

I had rented the wing of a fine house, standing on a wooded slope. The rooms were spacious, and there was a wide veranda, shaded with tall shrubs, and commanding a view down an avenue of planes leading to one cf the ancient gates of the city.

The deluge of water and the tremendous storms with which the rainy season opens, kept me prisoner for a considerable period. In my white apartments I dwelt as if in a drum, which was continually being beaten by a ruthless hand, as the silvery streams of tepid water lashed the window panes. At night the sky blazed as with Bengal lights. The crackling of the discharges and the deafening roll of the thunder dulled the senses, until dread gave place to resignation, in which the universe tarried as under the flaming sign of the last judgment, while, all around, houses and trees, struck by lightning, flared until the flames died down. This lasted for several weeks; the heat was still intense; so low were the impenetrable clouds that the sultry exhalations of the earth that had been baked for long months could find no egress. The lungs were choked with the heat and moisture of the supersaturated air. The atmosphere was like that of a forcing house. The last remnants of vital energy oozed away.

The vegetation, however, began to sprout with awe-inspiring luxuriance. At the end of a week, the house was darkened by the growth of the shrubs, until Panya had made a vigorous onslaught with his axe. When the lightning flashed in the night-time, in the blue shimmer there showed and vanished moment by moment a swathy interlacement of leaves, forming as it were an irregular and fluttering palisade outside the window. After the weather had grown calmer, it was a surprise to me to find that the town of Mangalore was still in existence.

Slowly, under the persistent rain, the temperature fell. No words can describe my feeling of elation, when the sun shone once more through the palm trees. The Indian spring had come again, and the heart, charmed with a thousand odours, could not conceal its exaltation.

Mangalore was blossoming like a flower of rainbow hues —exuberant, mysterious, silent, poisonously sweet in its avidity for life. Its fragrance brought oblivion; its murmur, nameless dreams of the complexity of the world; its colours, entrancement. A creeper thrust itself like a green snake over the balustrade of the veranda. Betwixt darkness and dawn, this burst into immense blue flowers. In the heart of each flower was a yellow, greedy eye, which allured the butterflies in the daytime and closed every night. The smell of the jasmine intoxicated me; the plaintive snore of the toads came as a pedal-bass to the joyous, metallic counterpoint of the nightingales; in the moonlight the lotus flowers gleamed from the black waters of the ponds and marshes.

The white-robed, brown-skinned figures of the natives, as they glided through the greenery along the red roads, moved like the unapproachable shapes of a fable conceived at a date long prior to that when our own people,

AN INDIAN JOURNEY

cradled beneath the oak trees of the remote west, had begun to live in the most ancient of our sagas. And with the other blessings, sleep, coming like a youth from a meadow glittering with dew, at length revisited my couch, and in his company came the happy consciousness of health, energy, and the joy of life.

XII · WOMEN, MISSIONARIES and BRAHMINS · XII

ANIFOLD and motley, therefore, were the impressions of the first months of my sojourn in Mangalore. Though I eagerly sought to discern a meaning in them, the general impression was one of confusion. A happy condition of well-being is apt, especially in youth, to incline us rather to unreflective gratification than to meditation. I therefore allowed the polychrome images to float past my eyes, feeling like a blithe traveller through changing scenes; and few of my experiences sank deep into my heart prior to the day when Mangeshe Rao set foot into my house.

Panya's high spirits seduced me into merry trifling. Two idlers were we on the quay, watching the activities of the port, which grew more bustling from day to day. Taking boat in the hunt for marsh birds, we threaded the river channels that seemed ten times as wide as on the day of our arrival. Now we risked our lives and now our money, forgetting sometimes that there were any other things in the world but the green and flowery wilderness and the gay town.

In front of the temples and in the bazaar there were pagan festivals on view. Brawls would occur at the harbour between the Mohammedans, Hindus, and the negroes who came from Arabia in sailing ships to trade in spices. It was amusing to share in the life of the party, alternately dull and exciting—leaving to Providence and the British government the care for my own well-being and for that of my new associates. I struck up an acquaintance with negroes, elephants, and kings, for in Mangalore there is a generous supply of all three. The spring was lavish with its gifts of intoxication, forgetfulness, and fervour. The sun-kissed stream of existence that flooded the whole city carried us on its current.

Lapped in the mysteries of this strange world, refreshed by the blissful clearness of the sunshine, and guided by youth's untiring love of life, my days succeeded one another. The last of my books had been devoured by the insects; my thoughts were the booty of dreams; and even my hopes for the future were long forgotten amid the gentle allurements of pleasures that were no less ephemeral than absorbing. I was awakened in the mornings by the shafts of the sun thrusting into my room through the flowers and palm fans of the garden, or by the aroma of tea which Panya brought to my bedside; and my first craving was for one of those green cigars of the country, thick and long as asparagus grown in a hot-house, and made of the choicest leaves. The golden days were spent in butterfly hunts or in boating expeditions; in the fresh sea air or in the deep shade of the palm groves; among men wise or foolish, or among beasts; on horseback or afoot—but always in that indescribable elation which arises from the consciousness that, whether one is respected or feared, one is at any rate regarded as something quite out of the ordinary. Thus were the hours spent until the cool of evening came, and the busy hum of men was silenced; until the ghostly lights of the great fireflies began to flit through the air, and the stillness of the night was broken by the love-calls of the beasts. I shall not trouble to tell my readers whether I was alone or companioned during the brilliant moonlit nights. Many are squeamish about such matters, and an author should never hurt anyone's susceptibilities, least of all by the record of his own joys.

In this realm of adventure, Panya got into serious trouble, and one morning he poured out his heart to me. He appeared with two long scratches running down one of his cheeks, and the origin of these was all the easier to guess since he had spent the night away from home.

Noting, as he prepared breakfast, that my eyes were riveted on his face, he said dolefully:

"Terrible thorns, Sahib! One can't avoid them in the dark. It's time I cleared the garden once more."

We exchanged complaints about the thorns for a brief space. Then I said:

"Sometimes two of them grow close together, just like finger-nails."

Panya eyed me suspiciously; but, since I did not smile, he rejoined:

"Yes, they grow in all sorts of ways."

At this my face must have betrayed me, for he stumped the floor angrily, and exclaimed:

"So you know what's the matter, really! But why should you tease me about it? It is unkind to make fun of me when you can see I've had the worst of it."

I murmured a few words of condolence. He was greatly put out, and was far from admitting that he could himself be in anyway to blame for his troubles. In fact he grew melancholy, as good-natured folk with an uneasy conscience are apt to do when others are blamed for their own peccadilloes.

"Do the women of your country use their nails too?" he enquired, assuming me to be a person of experience.

"Of course, Panya. They scratch themselves, and other people."

"Please be serious," he pleaded. "I am talking quite seriously, and when I was trying to go to sleep I was turning the matter over in my mind."

"Why don't you get married?" I asked.

There was silence for a moment. The cries of the chafferers in the bazaar came to our ears, and the twigs of the bushes were shaken by some big beast on its morning prowl.

"I suppose that's a monkey," said Panya, who was obviously thinking of something else. Suddenly he burst out: "Well, suppose I marry, what then? When one is still young it is not very attractive to know what is waiting

AN INDIAN JOURNEY

for one in one's bed. Curiosity and danger are necessary to love; and love without obstacles is like a caged bird."

I made up my mind to treat the matter more seriously, and therefore I said lightly:

"If the only thing in the world were what you now mean by love, Panya, you would be right. But it may happen that everywhere the heart feels like a caged bird, and not only where a particular woman is waiting."

Panya reflected for a moment.

"It comes, Sahib, but it passes."

"Perhaps something else may take its place?"

"What should that be, Sahib?"

"A son, perhaps."

"Oh, no," said Panya in consternation. "Why think of the worst? Even if I were to take pleasure in such a thought, how can I think of a son when I have none?"

"Is it better to forget, or to remember, Panya? Look around you in nature, and at the life of man. Always you will find love associated with remembrance, and depravity with forgetfulness. Is not a child the most beautiful token of love? Is it not the most charming companion on the way from summer to autumn?"

Panya plucked at his turban, and scratched himself pensively. This was always a sign that I had said something which passed his understanding, but he would not as a rule vouchsafe any other intimation of the fact.

"I'm not a Brahmin," he said at length. "Why should I trouble my head about these questions? The only reason you have such fine thoughts, Sahib, is because you know nothing of women. When you have a wife of your own, you'll think otherwise."

I could not but laugh, and Panya was triumphant. It was his turn to instruct me.

"Maybe the women of your country are different, Sahib; but I expect that woman is like the palm tree, the same all over the world. Did you ever notice that at bottom they are all equally stupid? For instance a woman is no more afraid of a tiger than she is of a mouse; the reason is that women cannot really recognise any difference between these two beasts. In the same way, women cannot recognise the difference between men; and the one they love, always seems to them the best."

"Is not that a merit?"

But Panya would not be turned from the thread of his discourse.

"If you say something utterly stupid, they stare at you in delight, simply because your words are of absolutely no importance. But if you say something really clever, something that all the sages would admire, they forget it in an instant because it is not a thing they can pick up and stick in their hair. Their ways are amazing! As time passes, perhaps your love wanes, and you become a reasonable being once more. Thereupon the woman grows passionate in proportion as your own passion cools. She decks you out, like a wonder-working idol, with everything she can imagine or discover, so that you begin to think so much of yourself that you make other men laugh at you. But what are you to do when your heart cleaves to her more and more fondly, and when you are met with increasing coldness for your pains? Do you give her all that you have, and throw yourself unreservedly into the bargain? Your mistress will promptly begin to make eyes at other men. The soul of such women is like a pit which grows smaller the harder you work at it, so that there is no end to the troubles you are laying up for yourself. You cannot imagine what even the best of men have to suffer in this respect! You said once that no one grows poor through giving; but what is given to a heartless woman, is lost for ever."

"Perhaps so, Panya. But not all women are heartless."

"Sahib, as long as we are still in love with a woman, everything in her seems beautiful," answered Panya with conviction. "This evil in her serves only to inflame our passion."

Panya went on to describe at greater length the miseries of mortal men: of those who love; of those who wish to love and cannot; and of those who love in spite of themselves. I was sparing in my comments, while turning over in my mind how many men there are of my own age and country who never get further than such views of women. Panya's ideas had all the simplicity of a child's; but underlying them was an outlook with which I was perfectly familiar. Yet it seemed to me futile to contradict him, because I recalled his youth and because I remembered that most men have to learn by experience, and that no one's experience can be greater than he himself. Besides, such views as Panya's may help kindly youngsters to practise as much caution as they are capable of.

Nevertheless it is a pity, in one's outlook upon sex, to

remain a child too long; and I have always found it difficult to avoid laughing at men who, because a woman's mind does not necessarily work in the same way as a man's, refuse to admit that a woman can have a mind of her own. When a thing is hidden, only the superficial will jump to the conclusion that it does not exist. How absurd, too, it is to blame women for the possession of qualities which we cannot praise too highly as long as we find them useful to ourselves. The more definitely a woman's emotional and intellectual life combines with her individual qualities to endow her with character, the more certainly will she be able without previous experience to make a choice which is accordant with her own worth. But after her decision, this worth will show itself, not in her capacity to compare men justly one with another, but in her constancy.

While morning after morning was spent in gossip and light-hearted trivialities, the sun of this happy region was again beginning to excel us mortals greatly in constancy, fidelity, and power. As doubtless happens to many others who are travelling, I found myself, in the superfluity of holiday freedom, often craving for that severe assurance of a higher freedom within the spirit which is accorded us when we are using our best energies to the full. But under a tropical sun it is not possible for men of our race to turn to the greatest advantage that race's peculiar aptitudes. Least of all is it possible to give free rein to our inclination towards steady work. Since the dawn of history, countless Europeans have succumbed to the tempta-

AN INDIAN JOURNEY

tions of the southern sun; who, almost without knowing it, have surrendered passively to the sweets of idle enjoyment; and after paying forfeit of their vital energies, have been scared into a revival of active home-sickness—whereas previously, throughout the languorous days, their feelings had not risen in intensity above the level of a voluptuous melancholy. Often, as I lay on the beach in the shade, my dreams and my volitions see-sawing between the blue of the water and the blue of the sky, I thought of Homer and of his hero. I thought of Odysseus, tied to the mast of his ship, but with his senses free; impotent, and racked with longing, as his ship sped by the isle of his desire; knowing, and made invulnerable by knowledge; given lordship by reason which was older than his yearning. Many times did I envy him, and many times did I sympathise with him, as one whom the coldness of his intellect had banished from the altar of blessed surrender. But the sirens appeared to me also in my dreams, and behind the charm of their alluring bodies I could discern the death-dealing power of their murderous claws.

Driven from one thing to another under the spell of an inward restlessness, I tried to work, but could not get beyond poor beginnings, and speedily burned my awkward attempts to embody the surrounding splendours in words and images. When the sun kindled its green-and-gold morning fires in the bushes outside my window, I was overwhelmed by a perfection before which all human effort seemed nil, gaudy, and perishable. The only solace left was devout contemplation.

AN INDIAN JOURNEY

Panya watched me solicitously, and one day he enquired:

"Sahib, why don't you burn the paper before you write on it?"

This annoyed me. A servant is not entitled to ask such questions!

"Idiot," I said, "don't you know that one can write one's thoughts on a sheet of paper, and that when words and paper are burned together, the thoughts rise in the smoke and make their way into the heads of persons whom we want to bring over to our way of thinking?"

Panya stared at me open-eyed, and meditated in silence. This was news to him. Not long afterwards I spied him in the garden strangely gesturing as he burned a letter. I stole away well pleased, for I knew that frustrated hopes would pay him out for his irreverent question.

Now and then I came in contact with the members of the German mission in Mangalore, earnest and energetic folk, whose main activity appeared to be the organising of small industrial employments for the converts. Rarely, and always fruitlessly, did they venture to struggle on the intellectual plane with the cultured representatives of Hinduism. For such a task their own intellectual equipment was inadequate. Above all, their contempt for Brahminism and Buddhism, their simple conviction that these doctrines were the outcome of "pagan blindness," was the best way to ensure failure. I encountered some queer creatures among the men and women attached to the mission. Fatal to their aspirations is the way wherein they deliberately restrict themselves within the outlook of a philosophy whose effective potentialities still remain a matter for doubt. It is so easy to be sure we are right when our only critics are those of the same way of thinking as ourselves; and the pity of it is that, while the missionaries' simplicity is associated with a certain nobility of mind, their prudence is characterised by want of tact.

Typical of such persons is their capacity for discussing and appraising all subjects under the sun, without having taken the trouble to understand them. Naturally, therefore, they are apt to note the seamy side of whatever comes under their observation; for both in things and in men this seamy side is conspicuous to a superficial observer, and requires no skill for its detection. As a rule, therefore, their sense of self-importance leads them to concentrate their attention upon the less favourable characteristics of brethren from whom they differ, and of things and persons with whom their kinship is more remote. Often enough, they can discern nothing but the seamy side. Hence their self-complacency finds continual nourishment, and grows rankly. Panya said one day, when we had exchanged a few visits with the missionaries:

"These Sahibs are like the king of Shamadji. They are always on the throne, but no one knows why, and they have practically no subjects."

Unpretentious people do not demand thanks for what they have done; and it is always rather distressing to see servants preening themselves because masters have achieved something great. Nevertheless, a proof of the staunchness of their faith came under my notice. I should be sorry if the foregoing remarks upon the missionaries

AN INDIAN JOURNEY

should cause me to be classed among those who hold them up to ridicule, so I will tell the following story.

At a prayer meeting held by this small, Christian community, one of the missionary women took up her parable. She hailed from a remote corner of the kingdom of Wurtemburg, and her holy zeal was tempered with a very scanty measure of discretion. After a brief prayer, as is the custom in such gatherings, she went on to say that God, in his inscrutable wisdom, had been pleased to afflict with a tapeworm her daughter Helene, a grown-up damsel sitting beside her. She then asked the congregation to join with her and her daughter in fervent supplications for the expulsion of the unpleasant parasite. All present were perfectly willing, and for a considerable time the prayer meeting was busied with petitions concerning the young lady's tapeworm.

At the close of the meeting, a kind-hearted woman among those present remarked that she had in her medicine chest a drug which would probably be too much even for the most vigorous of tapeworms, and the offer of a dose was gratefully accepted. At the very next meeting, the mother was able to report to the attentive congregation that their united prayers had been graciously answered. Her voice trembling with emotion, she explained that at the time of its discharge the intruder seemed already to have entered upon its last sleep, and that its appearance was one of perfect peace. . . .

A missionary of long experience, a war-worn veteran in the service against the heathen, told me another story, no less remarkable, and affording a no less convincing proof of God's keen interest in the well-being of these self-sacrificing residents of Mangalore. One lovely evening, in the early days of his missionary career, my informant was sitting on the veranda of his house. Suddenly he caught sight of a tiger, walking up the steps out of the garden. God, however, sent the alarmed missionary a thought which rescued him from peril. On the veranda, fortunately, was a harmonium, which had been left there since the last Sunday-school class. (These helps to edification, which are so greatly loved in pious circles, do not thrive in the climate of India, but some of the missions use them none the less.) In his extremity, the missionary sprang to the harmonium and, firm in the faith, began to play the well-known and beautiful hymn-tune,

> How shall I receive you,
> And how your coming greet?

The tiger promptly turned tail and sought his lair in the jungle.

One afternoon a trader from Cashmir had spread out on the veranda for my inspection his stock of brass pots and gay embroideries. At this moment a messenger from the town arrived. After the manner of native servants, he stood diffidently at the foot of the steps, waiting for me to speak to him. So many unimportant messages used to arrive for Panya or the cook, that I paid no particular heed to the new-comer. After a time, he hemmed discreetly; and when I looked up at him he placed his hand

AN INDIAN JOURNEY

on his forehead and bowed once more. His message was to me, then. I beckoned to him, saying:

"You've turned up just at the right moment. You have no axe to grind. Tell me how much you think that curtain stamped in gold is worth."

The messenger carefully examined the stuff and the work. It seemed to me that he was trying to discover a middle course which would be just both to me and to the trader. Then he said:

"I know little about the value of such things, but I am well acquainted with this merchant, Devan Chundar, and I know him to be an honest man."

"Were he otherwise, he could learn honesty from you," I remarked, delighted with the answer.

I looked at the new-comer more attentively. He was well dressed, strictly in the native fashion. His turban was made of red silk; he wore a voluminous, white loin-cloth, reaching down to the knee and looking like a pair of wide breeches. Chest and arms were covered by a short jacket of dark cloth, such as the Parsees wear in Bombay.

"What is your errand?" I enquired.

"My master wishes me to tell you that he thanks you for your message, and that he hopes to call on you at this hour to-morrow."

"Do you serve Mangeshe Rao, the Brahmin?"

"My master is Bahadur Mangeshe Rao."

I dismissed him with a silver rupee. My heart was thumping with joyful expectation. Though I had feared I might be wasting my pains, I had followed the Collector's advice, and had written to the Brahmin to ask whether he would be willing to give me lessons in Sanskrit and in the history of India. During the last few weeks I had been inclined to fear that through my frivolous doings in the town I might have forfeited all chance of winning the confidence of a man interested in the graver aspects of politics and diplomacy. I had become rather conspicuous, for my behaviour was so utterly different from that of the English residents, and I certainly did not take the missionaries for my model. Apart from civil servants and missionaries, there were very few Europeans in Mangalore. Panya had told me a number of amusing stories concerning what was generally thought of me among the natives. Some fancied I must be a spy in the service of the British government; others regarded me as a dealer in pearls; the common people looked on me as a sorcerer, because on one occasion I had shown off in friendly competition with a juggler, who had never seen a pack of cards before, and who knew no more of card tricks than I knew of snake charming.

It appeared, however, that Mangeshe Rao had not been estranged by my reputation. I gave the trader the price for which he had asked, and the man spent the rest of the day carefully packing up his wares. Obviously, the stroke of business he had done that morning would enable him to retire into private life for a few weeks. I called Panya.

"I know all about it," he said frigidly. "You are going to entertain criminals. We shall all three be hanged soon."

"How do you know who is coming?"

"You told me yourself, Sahib."

AN INDIAN JOURNEY

I was sure that I had done nothing of the kind, and yet I could not answer for myself. Again and again I was astonished anew by some proof of the minuteness with which all my doings were scrutinised; but eavesdropping is the most sacred duty of an Indian servant, and I felt sometimes as if my life depended upon my discretion. This much was certain, that Panya was hostile to my making the Brahmin's acquaintance. He had poured into my ears all the slanders and suspicions which have accumulated to the discredit of the Brahmin caste during the last two thousand years. Nevertheless, in Panya's manner, I could detect unmistakable signs of alarm. He could not free his mind from the veneration which all other castes feel for the Brahmins, a veneration which persists in spite of hatred and fear.

Mangeshe Rao arrived next day, precisely at the appointed hour. Riding through the garden gate, he dismounted at the wooden steps of the veranda. The sais announced his master with a soft call, ceremonious and impressive, which is indelibly stamped upon my memory. Panya now appeared with a grave and dignified mien.

I met my visitor as he mounted the steps, and he held out his hand to me in the European fashion. The only point in his behaviour which recalled his caste to my mind was the ritual solemnity with which he put off his shoes before crossing the threshold, that he might tread the stranger's house with naked feet. He had no occasion to stoop. The shoes, saffron in colour, were as easy to remove as sandals, and seemed to slip off as if by magic.

AN INDIAN JOURNEY

It is unlikely that my guest realised what an impression his appearance made on me from the very outset. However great a man's reasonable self-esteem, he will always be restrained from an unqualified belief in his own prestige by the knowledge that he will be judged according to the experience of his merits—and the Brahmin certainly had no reason to suppose that, before seeing him, I had formed a peculiarly high opinion of these. When I learned his age, I was amazed at the youthfulness of his looks. This appearance of youth did not solely depend upon the fact that he was clean shaven and had a very narrow face. Contributory causes were the slenderness of his figure and the grace of his movements, about which there was nothing artificial. His dark eyes contrasted with the light brown of his face, and this again with the yellow of his silk turban. The first time my gaze encountered his, I was overwhelmed by a rush of desire, gratification, and pride. I sensed the presence of the spirit of the ages, which seemed to have crowned the temples of this latter-day descendant with the halo of its own culture. Youthful dreams in which the name of India had conveyed a mysterious charm were blissfully reawakened; and my feeling was that to-day, at long last, the door of India's secrets was to be opened to me.

During the first words of our conversation, he looked at me as if nothing were further from his thoughts than any desire to pry into my soul. Never before had one of commanding intelligence exhibited this modest self-restraint towards me. I realised how much trepidation, aggressiveness, and false solicitude, underlie the scrutiny—

AN INDIAN JOURNEY

active or passive—which is apt to mark the opening stages of a new acquaintanceship. The lack of a prying cast in his eyes was gratifying. It diffused a sense of ease, as if nothing in the world could be more natural than our meeting. I recalled the Collector's story, and could not but smile at the picture he had endeavoured to arouse in my mind. I knew, of course, what lay at the root of the Englishman's trouble, and was keenly delighted that the interests which had brought the Brahmin and me together were outside the realm of politics.

I suppose this is why I was able to talk to him without reserve, with no unworthy circumspection, and with a frank serenity; and this is why he was quick to notice that the only thing I was afraid of losing was his personal esteem. I was amazed to note how accurately he appraised my mentality from outward manifestations. It was plain that, without dissimulation, or any excess of watchfulness, he was engaged during the first half hour of our interview in a quiet study of me, and that the result of his examination completely reassured him. We talked of the British government, and he praised it for its far-sightedness. Next the conversation drifted to the German mission; and, inasmuch as I was the missionaries' fellow-countryman, Mangeshe Rao's courtesy led him to dwell on their better side.

Being still rather young, I was inclined to resent being classed with these prophets of holy simplicity as one of the representatives of the German realm in India, so I remarked:

"They are a simple-minded crowd."

AN INDIAN JOURNEY

"That is not incompatible with their being honest," opined Mangeshe Rao.

I could not forbear the rejoinder:

"They cannot have done you much harm, since you are so indulgent towards them!"

Mangeshe Rao smiled, as if my indiscretion amused him. Then he gaily remarked:

"Oh, I just meet them on their own ground."

His opinion of the Jesuits was very different from his estimate of the Protestant missionaries. From the way he indicated that the activities and peculiarities of the Jesuit fathers had a certain kinship with his own aspirations, I was quick to perceive that he cared little for anything that lay without the realm of the spirit.

Not a word that had yet passed between us had indicated that my guest was in the least interested in politics, or even that he felt the slightest concern in the welfare of India, or in its economic and social condition. I began to wonder whether the Collector had made a mistake, and whether what he had regarded as a marvellous piece of acting in his reputed opponent had been anything more than a manifestation of perfect innocence.

The sunlight was playing with the objects in the quiet room. My guest sat in a shady corner, and as I watched him I was full of the genial pride of one who is entertaining a distinguished stranger. The blue curtain I had bought on the previous day now decked the wall of the room. It served as background to the visitor's figure, setting off his shoulders, his glossy, black hair, and the dull yellow of his turban, in a manner that conveyed a strange impression of unreality, so that at times I felt as if I were contemplating a picture from the fabulous world of the Arabian Nights. Now Panya silently entered, bringing tea and tobacco. I was positively startled to note the boy's profound and ceremonious obeisance to the Brahmin. Mangeshe Rao expressed his acknowledgments by a glance, without even bending his head.

After a while, my guest seemed to feel that we were getting on a little too fast with our questions and answers. Indians of mark have a definite routine for their intercourse with Europeans, and in their relations with the rulers of the country they practise the art of employing speech as a means to conceal thought. One may reasonably suppose that this art dates from an earlier epoch than their struggles with the English or even the Mohammedan conquerors, for the Hindus have suffered so many disappointments that they are extremely suspicious. When I got to know Mangeshe Rao better, candour proved more natural to him than dissimulation, but at this early stage of our acquaintance he was continually scrutinising my observations in search of a hidden meaning. Hence he would often hesitate, or be silent for a time; and I soon realised that the best way of gaining his confidence quickly was to show that I had no reserves on my side. But anyone to whom caution has become second nature, will, when his interlocutor's manner is exceptionally frank, be apt to wonder whether this frankness may not mask some ulterior design. Mangeshe Rao adroitly chose a means which gave him an opportunity for watchful silence. With an assumption of absent-

AN INDIAN JOURNEY

mindedness, he picked up a chess-board from an adjoining table, laid it down between us, and arranged the pieces.

We began to play. The game was exhilarating, but it did not last long. After my fourth move, my opponent, with civil regret, prophesied my inevitable defeat, and enquired upon which square I should prefer my king to be checkmated. I pointed to one of the squares, and the king, hemmed in by his own retainers and continually threatened by the foe, was driven like a chidden coolie from refuge to refuge, until at length, attacked by an enemy pawn from the rear, he met his inglorious fate upon the very square I had indicated.

"You played with my king much as you played with the Collector," I said, laughing.

Unhesitatingly Mangeshe Rao answered:

"Do not make too much of that little matter with the Collector. Perhaps some day I will tell you more about it."

"Then you don't mind admitting that you wrote the book?"

"What I admit between ourselves, I can just as easily deny when a third person is present. But can you suppose that I run any danger from a government which lacks courage to put a direct question, from fear lest the answer should compel it to prosecute? My shield was not my own adroitness. Half of that adroitness was no more than forbearance towards the person who was no match for it. The things that shield me are the power and the will of all those who are of the same way of thinking as myself."

AN INDIAN JOURNEY

"You know, then, that I have more than once visited the Collector?" I enquired, keenly interested.

Mangashe Rao nodded assent.

"In Mangalore it is easier for us to watch a European than for a European to watch us. At first I weighed the possibility that your letter to me might be inspired by the British government. That is why I came to see you. But the government has nothing to do with the matter."

"What guarantee have you of that?"

"Your parade of innocence," said the Brahmin with a smile. "Only the innocent make such a parade."

I could not help smiling; but as he remained serious, I asked:

"Suppose you are mistaken; or suppose that, merely in a spirit of idle gossip, I retail your admission to the Collector?"

"You will earn no thanks, and you will do me no harm," replied the Brahmin, with absolute indifference. "When a man knows something already, he is little interested in hearing it for the tenth time."

I passed the rest of the day in recounting to Mangeshe Rao all my experiences in India. I did not speak only of outward happenings, but also of the feelings which had sent me in search of them. He listened with tranquil mien, interjecting now and again a query which showed his sympathy, and moved me to increasing candour. At length I revealed to him the real reason why I had begged him to visit me, and it was with pleasure not unmixed with pride that in his courteous way he assured me that the best of his spiritual possessions were at my disposal.

AN INDIAN JOURNEY

"I fully understand the feeling that has driven you forth to wander," he said as he bade farewell. "Among all peoples, a few individuals are seized with this restlessness. Nowhere can they find repose, and they mingle with the world. Weal or woe goes with them; and whether weal or woe, depends on the measure of their value. Some are spurred by plenty, others by dearth. These latter imagine that they return home enriched; wherever they go, disorder and confusion follow in their train; and in reality they come back as empty as they went, for in vacant heads there is no room for anything. But the richly endowed give while seeking, and often the urge that goads them redounds to the advantage of those whom they encounter on their pilgrimage."

XIII·THE LAST FIRE AND THE OLD SPIRIT·XIII

THIS was still in the days of the "Prabuddha Bharata," India Awakened. The harbingers of the great spiritual current, moving far and wide throughout the land, had aroused in the minds of the Indians a new faith in the unification of the peoples under the light of their ancestral creed. The influence of the Brahma-Samaj (Society of God), founded in 1830 by Rammohun Rao, interpreting the Vedas and especially the Upanishads in the sense of an enlightened theism, transcending the darkness of idolatry and superstition, had initiated a movement towards social reform. This movement subsequently found expression in a vigorous campaign against the tyranny of caste. Towards the close of the nineteenth century, the name of Swami Vivakananda rang like a call to arms through the torpid and oppressed land; but the smouldering fires of this new truth never flashed heavenwards freely with the vigour of implicit faith.

AN INDIAN JOURNEY

These prophets of upheaval had successors. Adherents of the various trends aggregated into factions, only so that what had begun as a movement for unification under the sign of a reinvigorated national religion, degenerated into exhibitions of quarrelsome sectionalism. When, further, European agitators joined in the fray, the masses grew increasingly distrustful. Some of the thought currents began to flow in Buddhist channels; others came to exhibit the influence of Christian ideas; and British policy, well aware that the integrity of its own power was enhanced by dissensions among the peoples of India, adroitly took advantage of the situation by playing off the opposing factions one against the other.

The natural outcome of all this was that the conceptions of reform which had been originally directed towards the foundation of a renovated national church, began more and more definitely to assume a political aspect. The more fanatical adherents of the movement soon came to look upon it as an instrument for the freeing of the country from the British yoke. Therewith the essence of the whole matter was fatally corrupted, and nothing was left but the futile multiplicity of a nationalist movement rent by passionate dissensions.

I first learned of these things from Mangeshe Rao the Brahmin, whose sincere belief in the possibility of a united India fascinated me, as also did his antagonism to England. Our intimacy progressed; he grew ever more open in the expression of his feelings. I won his confidence as soon as he became convinced of my sympathy. Although he was careful to withhold details from me (being guided

AN INDIAN JOURNEY

here rather by principle than by any fear lest I should betray his trust), I soon acquired a broad general understanding of the political struggles of contemporary India.

He assumed that I would be more interested in his ideas than in the means by which he hoped they would be realised, and he left to me the task of drawing conclusions regarding the possibility of moving from the sphere of thought to the sphere of action. I found his love for India most inspiring. His hopes were ardent and youthful in their vigour, contrasting strangely with the indifference and self-command which it suited him to display towards the world. I learned to love him for the fervour and unselfishness with which he devoted himeslf to a cause whose significance and prospects I was not then in a position to judge. Unquestionably my facile enthusiasm might readily have involved me in grave complications.

The things which the Brahmin conveyed into the political struggle out of his richly stored world of splendid ideas, were no less closely connected with his youth, than his zeal was connected with his hopes. Essentially, he was anything but a politician, nor was he one whose interest the contentious questions of "mine" and "thine" could ever have monopolised for any considerable period. The priestly tradition of his caste, which with him was bred in the bone, continually recalled him to the tranquil realm of meditation; and abstract knowledge was far more important to him than the struggle for the glittering unrealities of ordinary life.

As I came to spend more time in the Brahmin's company, a change occurred in my manner of life, and I came to hold different views of the world that environed me. Alone and thoughtful, I would wander through the crowded bazaar, and past the dark entries of the temples, whence the plates of brass, affixed to the dusky wood that had been polished by the friction of countless hands and feet, gleamed mysteriously forth. I contemplated with a new understanding the manifold caste-marks on the foreheads of the natives, and learned to distinguish the various signs.

When the sound of drum or pipe or gong resounded from the obscurity of the temple courts, the notes had a fresh meaning for me after what I had learned from Mangeshe Rao concerning the significance of the various ceremonies. Now that I shared his hopes, I was inspired with the wish that the ancient spirit of the Hindu religion might free itself from the trammels of these pagan perversions, and regain its primitive freedom.

On one occasion we had walked far beyond the town limits along an avenue of palm trees until we reached the shore, conversing as we watched the naked Hindus, their brown skins glistening in the sunlight while they fished in the shallow waters. As so often happened, our conversation had turned from the secular domain of politics to religious questions. Hoping, perchance, to gain once for all a clear light as to the meaning of Hinduism, I asked Mangeshe Rao:

"What is Brahman? I listen to profound thoughts, to wisdom instinct with beauty, to ideas of salvation filled with a bright faith in freedom. But the central notion of Brahman is still veiled in mystical obscurity."

AN INDIAN JOURNEY

The Brahmin answered:

"The heart alone can understand the divine nature, but I will answer you in the words of the earliest Vedantic priests. They tell us that Brahman is the light of the spirit and the blessedness that knows nothing of sorrow. Brahman is joy, primal knowledge, a homogeneous mass of understanding, compact of beatitude, accessible through the consciousness, and equipped with supreme insight."

It was natural after this exposition, to enquire how the heart can share in all these benefits. Mangeshe Rao reflected for a space, and then rejoined:

"I will quote a passage from the Upanishads. It may not, perhaps, be a direct answer to the question as you have phrased it, but it would be the right answer to a rightly phrased question:

> "The pious man, acquainted with the true knowledge,
> Contemplates it with the eye of understanding,
> Knowing that in himself the whole universe is comprised,
> And that he himself is one and all.
> Like an iron ball that is permeated
> With fire, so does Brahman permeate
> The universe within and without
> With his light, which is self-luminous."

He spoke gently but solemnly. I felt as if a millenniary spiritual realm were recalling its vanished glories, and I was filled with a dark and mournful sense of the India that had passed out of ken. With secret anxiety I realised the futility of the struggle in which my friend was involved as if in an overwhelming doom, and my desires vacillated restlessly between the values of the old world and the new. Mangeshe Rao apparently guessed my thoughts, for after a brief silence he resumed in a tone that was almost matter of fact:

"It makes us heavy-hearted when we are forced to recognise that all the sacrifices we have made for the welfare of the enslaved people are fruitless, that all we have gained by these sacrifices becomes simply a fresh occasion for mistrust. When I decided to enter as a student at the University of Madras, I was expelled from the fellowship of my caste; and when subsequently I fought my way to an influential position in the enemy service, I forfeited the last vestiges of my intimates' confidence. But what other way is there in which we Indians can carry on the struggle against England? Here in India the government still suppresses freedom of thought; but ere long, in India no less than elsewhere, thought will enter into its own. Therewith will come the beginning of the end of British rule. The far-sighted among our conquerors are aware of this. Already there is manifest a strong trend in favour of limiting such rights as we already possess, for England knows where she is competent to encounter us and where she is outclassed. But it is, indeed, painful in such a struggle to find that our own fellow-countrymen, those on whose behalf we are fighting, themselves turn against us."

These words often came back to my mind after my friend's doom had been fulfilled. I recalled them as a definite foreshadowing of his own fate.

The sea was bright between the stems of the palm trees.

AN INDIAN JOURNEY

We had reached the burning-ground for the dead. A wood pile had been made ready for the evening now drawing on, and the body of the dead man, with limbs artificially broken and bent to a right angle, lay nude on the little scaffold. Heaps of ashes remained to mark the fires of previous days, and suddenly I remembered the strange odour of burning flesh I had noted on many evenings. Amid this reek, the souls merge into Nirvana. I scrutinised the face of Mangeshe Rao. Behind the tranquil forehead glowed the dread hope that soon revolt would be raging through the streets.

A leprous beggar crawled on all fours across the red road towards us. He had been hiding in the undergrowth to escape the stones thrown by his persecutors. Now he made raucous noises, as if driven insane by his sufferings, twisting his hideous head the while. A number of crows had settled on the beach, and their caws disturbed the sun-lit peace. I turned away after I had caught sight of the bones of a human thorax picked almost clean.

"Plague and smallpox are reaping their harvest," said Mangeshe Rao.

He was silent as we walked homeward. Like me, doubtless, he was oppressed by the thought of how numerous were the enemies by which his country was beset, enemies against whom struggle was of no avail. He was thinking of the ills that befall a nation that is decrepit and has grown weary—immorality, vice, poverty, and pestilence.

Panya still felt it his duty to caution me from time to time, and from his point of view he was right. I did my best to calm his fears, although in reality his concern was dependent rather upon jealousy than upon genuine apprehension.

"The British are afraid of my friend, Panya. Nothing worse than banishment is likely to happen to him, and if the same lot should befall me, it would suit my present plans well enough. We should probably travel to Bombay at State expense."

Panya's rejoinder was calm, and almost melancholy.

"You don't know this country, Sahib. Who said anything about danger threatening you or the Brahmin from the British? Don't you know that the priests of his own caste hate Mangeshe Rao as much as jackals hate the hyena? The weapons the Brahmins use stifle the cry in the victim's throat. In the depths of the palm grove there is a darkness which the eye of no judge can pierce. It is said of the cobra that we do not catch sight of it until we are already face to face with death, and to the Brahmin priests the cobra is sacred."

"What do you mean, Panya?"

I was seriously concerned, for when this strange and childlike friend of my Indian days spoke dispassionately, his words were worthy of credence. I had long been aware that his initial hatred of Mangeshe Rao had been transformed into an unacknowledged liking. This change had not cured him of jealousy, but it rendered me more attentive to his anxieties.

"I don't know," he answered. "But why should you run the risk? Who is there to protect you? You can only trust an Englishman as long as you are still useful to him; and if you are friendly with his enemy, he will no longer regard you as his own friend. Mangeshe Rao stands in the middle, where no one will support him. The priests and the government alike consider him a traitor. In the struggle for the country no one bothers, as you do, to study a man's heart."

"Panya, I care little for joys which can be secured without danger. What I win is worth the trifling stake."

"Don't think that I speak as I do because I want to leave you," answered Panya simply.

It was long since I had seen him in such deadly earnest, and I carefully pondered my position.

For the last few weeks Mangeshe Rao had visited me less often. There was a tense feeling in the atmosphere, and it was all the more impressive because the cause of the tension remained obscure. Nevertheless, in the hours we spent together my new friend's mood was often one of serene unconcern. In our diversified talks he laid aside the burden of his self-imposed tasks. One evening he was accompanied by a servant carrying the skin of a Siamese panther. This was a present from Mangeshe Rao, a memento; and for an instant I thought he meant it to be a parting gift. During the evening my eyes often rested upon the splendid black fur. With a thousand memories of the wilderness, the thought of the night surged up in my mind—the Indian night and the Reign of the Beast.

After nightfall, when we were sitting on the veranda, our talk turned upon the world's literature and its noted names. A cloud of insects was collecting within the circle of lamplight, and ere long the table resembled a battlefield after a fierce encounter. The mysterious night was full of the ardent love-plaints of countless tropical creatures, and the leaves glistened in the brilliant moonlight.

I was strangely moved when the name of Goethe, at this immense distance from the German poet's home, was pronounced as a matter of course, with the implication that his writings had long since become the spiritual property of the whole civilised world. The Brahmin's opinion concerning Goethe's achievements—an opinion which he counterposed to my own youthful enthusiasm—was sufficiently strange to remain for ever imprinted on my memory.

"Goethe," said Mangeshe Rao, "has become so predominantly the educator of the German people in mood and aspiration, that it is hard for you and your fellow-countrymen to appraise justly his educational influence. Most Germans look upon him as if they were looking out of his own eyes; and his authority has become so overwhelming that there is no independent standard by which he can be measured. Ultimately, however, like all great men, he will be classed in accordance with his creative power, and in this respect Friedrich Schiller seems to us the greater genius."

We spoke of Dante, whose lofty aims he extolled, and whom he loved above all other writers. We spoke of Shakespeare; and finally of Kalidasa, whose Sakuntala he esteemed more highly than any of the dramas of the great Englishman.

His views, and the reasons for them, gave me a strangely

AN INDIAN JOURNEY

new and generalised picture. I could not but smile, when I thought of all the "great writers" whom the parents of our generation, and we ourselves in youth, were so ready to rank with the immortals.

Panya was delighted next day when I told him I had decided to make a journey up country with Mangeshe Rao, and that he was to accompany us. It was to last for several days. We were to go close to Barkur, and to visit the Shita waterfalls.

I was sitting with Mangeshe Rao beside the fire, at the border of the virgin forest in the infinite night. The forest was full of voices, and these voices aroused in me a mood of passionate sorrow. Never have I seen the stars shine so brightly as on this memorable night, a night which has been indelibly impressed on my mind owing to the thoughts uttered on this occasion by my usually taciturn companion. Panya was already asleep in the tent, for this was his way when he felt that he was not wanted. Out of the shadows came the sound made by our oxen as they grazed, tearing off the grass with their teeth and snuffling along the ground. The moon had not yet risen, but the light of its imminent coming was visible on the horizon.

After supper, Mangeshe Rao had silently rolled and smoked a cigarette. To-night, as on so many others, we should certainly have gone to bed after exchanging no more than a word or two, had not a strange incident startled us. One of the oxen, which was still wearing part of its harness, suddenly began to shake itself in a peculiar fashion.

AN INDIAN JOURNEY

Mangeshe Rao instantly threw a couple of handfuls of brushwood on the fire, and this made me realise that the noise was of an unusual character. Tall tongues of flame rose into the night; for a brief space the blue expanse of heaven vanished; our immediate surroundings lighted up, and looked like a red room. Mangeshe Rao walked cautiously towards the beast, catching up his gun and carrying it at the trail as he peered into the darkness. I followed his example. Few of the dangers of India approach plainly in the open, so that few of them can be faced and awaited with perfect calmness. It is the brusque intrusion of peril on which depends in large measure the sense of eeriness which none can escape in the Indian wilderness except those whose perceptions are dull to all such intimations. What has impressed my imagination has not so much been this or that particular happening when my life or that of my friends was in danger. Upon the incomprehensible uncertainty of the menace did it depend that, even to-day, the sight of palm trees or the steamy atmosphere of a hothouse can thrill me with alarm. A palm leaf has become associated in my mind with the shadow of death, whereas I can contemplate the movements of a snake with no more emotion than that aroused by their beauty and strangeness. In Bombay, I was once attacked in a narrow alley by a Mohammedan native. The man fired at me, but this has not produced any trace of uneasiness either as regards fire-arms or as regards people of the Indian race. And yet for years afterwards the scarcely audible patter of naked feet upon a stone pavement would arouse a sense of horror. Almost the only memory that remains to me of the occurrence is the stealthy "pad, pad" which immediately preceded the onslaught.

In like manner, during this night in the jungle, the certainty that a panther or some other beast of prey was prowling round our camp would have been far less disturbing than was the vague expectation of the unknown, which seemed just as likely to reveal itself as something trifling or as something monstrous. Write me down a coward if you please!

We found one of our oxen convulsed and trembling, so that its harness rattled unceasingly. Vainly did we endeavour to drive the beast towards the fire, where there might have been light enough for us to discover what was amiss. Suddenly Mangeshe Rao warned me to stand perfectly still, but I was unable to follow his advice, for at this instant the huge animal sank noiselessly to the ground, and, after snorting and coughing for a few moments, was racked with terrible spasms and then died. The flame of the camp fire was subsiding, so that the starlight was again dominant. In this light the giant frame of the dead beast showed white upon the dark background of the grass, which stretched away far into the blue distance.

The Brahmin had his own notions as to the cause of this sudden death, and he now made a careful examination in order to confirm his suspicions. At length he discovered what he had expected. Making up the fire once more, by the light of the flames he showed me upon the muzzle of the ox a tiny puncture with dusky margins.

"There it is," he said; "the bite of a cobra."

I shuddered. As I contemplated the inert body lying

at my feet, as I thought of the suddenly quenched life, it seemed to me an irrelevant consideration whether the victim of the poison had been man or beast. Once again was I able to understand the Indians' veneration for the cobra. Mangeshe Rao's expression betokened this veneration, as if the enlightenment of his education had been unable to annul his ancestral respect for the dread deity.

Doubtless it was as the outcome of this experience that our conversation now turned to the topic of death. I will record what I can remember of the conversation. Once more we had seated ourselves beside the fire, which we kept burning throughout the night. Mangeshe Rao's habitual imperturbability had vanished for the nonce. He was strangely restless, and it pained me to watch the conflict between his acquired rationalism and the traditional philosophy of the priestly caste to which he belonged. No words can convey the clearness of the image I still have of him in my mind. I see his pensive countenance surmounted by the turban ruddy in the firelight; the slope of his delicate shoulders; his bowed head—for his eyes were fixed on the hands resting on his knees, as if he hoped to draw inspiration from this source. Among those with whom I have conversed concerning matters of moment, in one of those heart-to-heart talks between intimates, never have I known anyone display the mingled ease and frankness of Mangeshe Rao. He once said to me: "You must not make things simple for one with whom you are arguing by interrupting him, for this will often save him from displaying his own vacuity." Even when Mangeshe Rao was in an ironical mood, there was

AN INDIAN JOURNEY

no venom in his sallies. He never plumed himself upon a victory in debate, and he was especially genial when his interlocutor had sustained a defeat. Nevertheless, his silence could be wounding to those who realised that he was deliberately refraining from pushing a victory home.

In Mangalore, one day when I went to call on him, I found him sitting in the shade of the palm trees in front of the house, playing chess with a Jesuit father. He went on talking throughout the game, which he won. The Jesuit said that the conversation had been deliberately continued by the Brahmin in order to distract his opponent from the game, so a new game was begun upon the express condition that neither party was to say a word while it was in progress. The reverend father, who was still a trifle piqued by his defeat, could not refrain from adding: "If you find it possible to hold your tongue so long."

Mangeshe Rao made no answer, but silently arranged the pieces. After a few moves, the Jesuit lost his queen, and gave up the game. Thereupon Mangeshe Rao modestly remarked: "I only took your queen because it would have been ill-mannered to keep silence any longer in the presence of a lady."

That night I talked of death, somewhat emotionally at first, and from the romantic outlook of youth, for I had been deeply moved. Mangeshe Rao listened to me. When I had finished, he said:

"Do you hear the hungry hyenas howling?"

"Yes," I said, a trifle crestfallen.

AN INDIAN JOURNEY

He went on, in the unstudied way characteristic of those who are perfectly sure of themselves:

"What a banquet death has prepared for the hyenas! They will find the dead ox as soon as we have broken camp." Then: "I learned the meaning of death one summer day when, a stripling, harassed by painful thoughts and in the initial stages of a grave illness, I wandered forth from the town. Heavily, with fever in my veins, I walked among ruined habitations, through coarse grass, parched by the sun, which rustled beneath my tread. Suddenly I caught sight of a strange play of colours from between the fallen stones in the sunshine, and I could hardly believe my eyes when I saw a snake lying on the sand. I noted the splendid tints of the skin, tints ranging from the fierce sparkle of the diamond to the tranquil glow of the ruby, comprising, it seemed, all the colours of the rainbow. Entranced by the beauty and vigour of this dazzling spectacle, I eagerly moved a step nearer. There followed an angry hum. The radiant beauty of the sinuous body at my feet resolved itself into a motley swarm of insects rising into the heated air. Now I could see the putrefying remnants of a small grass snake. The delicate ribs showed here and there through the grey skin, and my nostrils were assailed by the sweetish and nauseating stench of carrion."

Tongues of flame from the camp fire between us were leaping upwards towards the star-bespangled heavens.

"I feel the truth underlying this parable, much as you may have felt it in actual experience," was my rejoinder.

AN INDIAN JOURNEY

"But that does not help me to co-ordinate with the assured touch of knowledge my thoughts concerning death."

"That last step towards the snake is what you need in order to reach assurance," said the Brahmin. "When you can tell me where life ceases and where death begins, I will explain death to you. Will you seek for the boundary among plants, human beings, stones, or the lower animals? Wherever I contemplate nature, I discern the renewal of all perishable forms. Life is manifest to me in the structure of the crystal. In the mathematical ordering of its molecules as it consolidates, I see something which appears to me intelligent as well as beautiful; something that manifests the working of the same laws as those in accordance with which I myself breathe, move to and fro, enjoy pleasure or suffer pain. Death is a vague assumption, which we are forced to make because of the temporal limitations of our faculties. As far as the individual consciousness is concerned, thoughts of death are ever more remote in proportion as we are immersed in the generality of all that is living. It is with death as with truth. Both are felt more keenly than any other elements of the living soul, but neither of them can be explained. There will always be two kinds of men: those who accept death as the duty of the individual creature; and those who look upon death as arbitrarily imposed by an external power. Your church teaches that death is the punishment for sin; but your God went to meet death as a voluntarily accepted duty, in atonement for sin."

"Do you, then, include Christ in your pantheon?" I en-

AN INDIAN JOURNEY

quired. "Do you think his life and thoughts find a place in your system of divinity?"

Mangeshe Rao answered:

"I can do this in so far as the essence of all earthly religions, or rather the religious sentiment of all mortals, flows from one source of aspirations; but I cannot do it doctrinally. The thoughts of Christ are greater than our thoughts, and lead further. Much has been said and written concerning the differences between the Christian religion and ours, and concerning the respects in which the two creeds resemble one another; but most of these comparisons are unmeaning. It is fruitless to compare fundamentally different types of phenomena. Brahminism is a philosophy; the wisdom of Christ is a practical doctrine. Those who are incompetent to grasp essentials are apt to dwell upon unimportant accessories, and to weigh these against one another. Their aim is usually to appreciate the one, and to depreciate the other. Perhaps my judgment is too harshly phrased. Let me say, then, that most of those who declare that thought is greater than feeling, or that understanding is greater than faith, are likewise prone to depreciate rather than to appreciate. To me, therefore, it is a matter of indifference whether Christ was familiar with the wisdom of the ancients. Great thoughts have never been young, and never grow old. They resemble one another as do the mountain summits above the snow line. The lower the levels we explore, the more differentiation shall we find. The mob is motley in its manifestations, and is uniform only in its wretchedness. But our goal is to be united in joy."

AN INDIAN JOURNEY

His utterance amazed and charmed me. In no spirit of contradiction, but ardently desiring to secure a fuller grasp of Mangeshe Rao's philosophy, I said:

"But how terrible has been the influence of Christ's teaching upon the human race. Must we not despair of Christianity even more than of any other creed, when we note the havoc that Christianity has wrought in the destiny of the nations?"

"Who proposes to ignore this influence?" enquired Mangeshe Rao. "What you speak of as the consequences of Christ's teaching seems to us no more than the first steps. I should describe the terrible and sanguinary struggles among men as to the meaning of Christianity, rather as the birth-pangs of the doctrine than as its outcome. Christianity is still in its infancy, and is far from being widely diffused as yet. Is it not an easy matter to trace its path upon the map, to show how it moved from Asia across Greece and Rome into the heart of Europe, as if this route had been traversed but yesterday? The domain inhabited by those who profess the Christian faith is not so large but that, with all its men, cities, and churches, it could be buried beneath the Himalayan massive. When the days since Christ's departure to now have been trebled, the kernel of his teaching will have shed the husks of the churches, and the full spiritual significance of Christianity will have been revealed."

The sun was rising in its majesty, as if hurled from abysses of everlasting fire. In the inconceivable triumph of its dominion, it was beginning another of its countless journeys across its earthly realm. The cries of the deni-

AN INDIAN JOURNEY

zens of the jungle were deafening, and the clamorous awakening of nature dispelled all thought of sleep. Picking up my gun, I strode across the open country, leaving the moist and teeming jungle behind. Amid the ardours that rise heavenwards when youth and morning meet, the words of Christ came into my mind: "I have not found so great faith, no, not in Israel."

XIV · · · · · · HOME! · · · · · · XIV

A FEW days after our return to Mangalore, the news ran through the town that political passion was greatly inflamed. The previous evening a draft of British troops had arrived. Ostensibly, they were sent for manœuvres, and to attend an official inspection of the province. But no one believed this innocent explanation. The most conflicting rumours were current. Knots of persons engaged in eager talk were to be seen in the bazaar and other public places. The unthinking mob, however, continued to go about its concerns as usual, regardless of the rights and duties of the government. As for the traders in the bazaar, these congratulated themselves at sight of the military uniforms.

The soldiers, in accordance with the regulations of that date, always went about in companies of four. With nonchalant mien, they stared open-mouthed at the incomprehensible peculiarities of the native city, amused themselves in careless fashion, and were so obviously at their ease that I was not inclined to pay serious heed to the alarmist reports.

Mangeshe Rao had not been to see me since our return. I had been greatly astonished, a few days earlier, when I caught sight of him driving with the English colonel. His features, on that occasion, had worn their usual impassivity. The British officer, in whose carriage the two were seated, was talking eagerly and gesticulating a good deal, but quite amicably. There was nothing to suggest that their companionship had any special significance.

Nevertheless, since this encounter, I had been uneasy, although on the face of the matter what I had seen ought to have reassured me. Apart from the fact that, generally speaking, political activities in India are peculiarly apt to wear a mask, this friendly visit of the British troops made me suspicious. The more I thought about it, and the more urgently I endeavoured to calm my apprehensions, the more ominous did it seem to me. An impression of furtiveness is aroused by the life of Hindustan, and this is eminently liable to cause disquietude and a sense of uncertainty. It seemed to me of a sudden as if all the things and persons around me were showing false colours. At one moment I mistrusted the Brahmin, greatly attached to him though I was; at another, I mistrusted Panya; at another, my own senses. I longed to escape from the entanglements of a life which I was unable to understand, and in which I had nevertheless become involved by my affection for Mangeshe Rao. In the end, I hailed with delight the strange opportunity that was

AN INDIAN JOURNEY

offered me, and recked little of the dangers into which I was being led; for I enjoyed the profound relief that comes to us when, after long hesitation, we take a decision.

My recent experience had convinced me that the Brahmin wielded more influence and was taken far more seriously than he had allowed myself or others to surmise. The realisation of this filled me with admiration and secret pride. I suppose that is why, almost unreflectingly, I acceded to Mangeshe Rao's request, the first and the last he ever made of me.

On a moonless night, towards two in the morning, Panya came to my bedside and awakened me by cautious hemming. The boy still retained his deferential method of announcing, and was especially gentle when he had to awaken me, for he knew that I was inclined to be peculiarly irritable at such times. It was so dark that I could make out nothing beyond the dusky, triangular opening in the white mosquito curtains. I could see no one.

"Why don't you get a light?" I asked, supposing Panya to be there. "What on earth do you want?"

"I may not get a light, Sahib. You must get up, please. A stranger wants to speak to you. He says that Mangeshe Rao the Brahmin, sent him."

It was Mangeshe Rao himself. Panya had advised me never to admit a caller who wanted to be received in the dark. But I thought that, after all, the visitor would see no more of me than I should see of him; and the use of my friend's name made me accommodating. The Brahmin wore an unfamiliar dress. At his request I dismissed Panya.

AN INDIAN JOURNEY

We sat facing one another, with a faint starlight coming through the window. I was just able to discern Mangeshe Rao's features. I fancied that his face was drawn and pale, but perhaps I was misled by the obscurity. It seemed to me that he was wrestling inwardly, half resolved upon an avowal, half desirous of saying a word concerning the anxieties of the last few days; but he did not refer to these things. After a period of silence, he said tranquilly:

"To-morrow the British soldiers will visit your house in search of evidence relating to a conspiracy which is supposed to be widespread, and to have supporters in Mangalore. As you know, I am a suspect, am believed to be of like way of thinking with the malcontents. Since I have been a frequent visitor here, it is thought that you may be involved in the affair."

"A conspiracy?" I said, startled.

Mangeshe Rao waited to see if I had anything more to say. For the moment, however, I was dumbfounded. I was confused and excited simultaneously by this nocturnal visit, by thoughts of the coming day, and of the disclosure that had just been made to me. How different is the aspect of things when viewed romantically from a distant outlook, and when they are close at hand.

"Conspiracies are every-day affairs in India," continued Mangeshe Rao, slowly and almost absently. "They are discovered and frustrated. Even if they are not discovered, nothing happens. The British officials must find some vent for their energies. It is the same on our side."

With a melancholy expression, he turned to look forth

into the night. Outside, the cicadas were singing. Two or three bright stars were visible, poised seemingly in the fanlike crests of the papaws.

"Unfortunately I have a good conscience," I said.

Never had this land seemed stranger and more alien to me. Being well acquainted with the Brahmin's habitual reserve, I was sure that what he had left unexpressed was more momentous than what he had said. Indeed, no words could have convinced me of the seriousness of the affair so effectually as did the mere fact of his nocturnal visit.

The previous day there had been a brief shower of rain. The window was open. Through the wooden bars a cool, scented air was wafted, murmuring softly as it made its way into the dark corners of the room. I felt as if I were dreaming.

"What can I do?" I asked.

From the bosom of his robe Mangeshe Rao took some packets tied with string. Their appearance suggested that they contained letters or other documents.

"Will you hide these papers for us?" he enquired calmly.

I assented without reflection—or rather, concerned only to wonder which would be the best hiding-place in house or garden. It never occurred to me for a moment to think that there must have been plenty of better hiding-places in Mangalore for a few incriminating documents. I was so profoundly impressed by the character of the man who asked this service of me, that I had no thought of the possibility that I might be made a tool of.

AN INDIAN JOURNEY

Since that date it has frequently occurred to me that young people who make such resolves as the one I made on this night are rarely actuated by any deliberate design. Often enough the thoughtless complaisance of a moment may have cost such as myself the loss of years of liberty, and may have involved the entire sacrifice of the most active period of life.

I took the papers. "Leave it to me," I said.

Then I recollected that my friend had just told me I was to expect a domiciliary visit on the morrow. Naturally, therefore, I asked for an explanation of the apparent inconsistency.

"I want these documents to be found here, in your house," said Mangeshe Rao.

He spoke in low tones, quite simply, and manifestly with no desire to envelope his commission in mystery. Those who are engaged on dangerous intrigues in India are well aware, not only that walls have ears, but that danger threatens everywhere—from the night, from a man's wife, from his most intimate friend. Understanding what the Brahmin was afraid of, I said:

"Panya is trustworthy."

Mangeshe Rao shook his head.

"He is a child. Good feeling and trustworthiness without discretion seem no better than treachery to those who know the enemies with whom they have to deal. You come from a country where frankness and strength are valued equally with boldness. Such qualities may become a free people. Our race has almost forgotten its freedom."

At these words I was seized with a sense of sadness in

AN INDIAN JOURNEY

which for the first time I grew fully aware of the affection I felt for Mangeshe Rao. I should have liked to urge him to withdraw from a fruitless and baleful struggle. It was plain to me that, notwithstanding the keenness of his intelligence, his opponents were too strong for him. The noble who struggle with the base are in the long run paralysed by disgust. But I said nothing, being overpowered by my veneration for the fire that burned in his breast.

Mangeshe Rao went on:

"Don't let the discovery be too easy, but make sure that the papers are found. Chance often takes a hand to counteract the most ingenious designs. Should the search party fail to happen upon what you want them to find, you can betray the documents by an apparently maladroit attempt to conceal them while the search is actually in progress."

He paused, as if expecting some objection, but I did not display the mistrust or anxiety which he seemed to anticipate. I was incapable of harbouring suspicion against my friend, and I know that he would never ask of me a service which might involve me in disaster. He now explained his reasons.

"Our time is not yet come," he said. "The papers which are to be found in your house are unimportant, and yet they are of such a character that the government will believe itself to be on the track of a notable discovery. Suspicion will be diverted, and the trail will be confused. The documents will be looked upon as a prize, and from them inferences will be drawn as to the extent of the intrigue. Some of our friends will be incriminated, but the punishment will not be serious, and they are willing to pay the price. Substantially, the authorities will learn nothing more than is already known to them."

"You are very frank," I rejoined, admiring the ingenuity of his plan.

"I give confidence for confidence," answered Mangeshe Rao, gazing at me for an instant with a cordiality unusual in this man whose features so rarely expressed any emotion.

I enquired what I was to say if I were asked how the papers had found their way into my house.

"Mention my name," said Mangeshe Rao.

"But what if you are prosecuted?"

"They will not venture upon that. The authorities will take proceedings against those only whom we have chosen to bear the brunt. I wish they would prosecute me, for this would inspire confidence in the persons for whom I am working. The more lenient the government is to me, the more inclined with the Brahmins of Mangalore be to consider me a renegade. Whether I openly attack the members of the priestly caste, or show forbearance towards them, I am just as liable to be misunderstood. It is far from easy to walk straight forward through a dark forest."

Another brilliant day dawned over Mangalore. Before the sun had tipped with gold the summits of the brown pagodas, I was riding through the swampy mangrove thickets along the lower reaches of the river, accompanied by Panya, who had a foreboding of danger and would not

AN INDIAN JOURNEY

let me out of his sight. The landscape, the animals, and the plants, all seemed strange to me. Beside a wooden shanty, a boat was moored on the dark waters. Squatting in this boat was a native, still drowsy, and shivering in the chill morning air as he stared out into the distance. I was reminded of the day I left Cannanore upon my pilgrimage through the jungle, and when, at Beliapatam, Panya had wrangled with the Mohammedan about the hire of the dug-outs.

As the light grew stronger, memories and images of this journey surged through my mind. I thought of its joys and sorrows, and of my never-ceasing desire to make this country my home, and to acquire those ties which lead through intimacy to love. Huc, the monkey of my vision, was once again seated in front of me, prophetic and wise, wearied by the hopes of suffering creatures—hopes which are as old as the destinies of the earth.

Was it the unrest, the hatred and bitterness of my new acquaintances, was it their petty and yet important interests, that had destroyed the faith in harmony which contact with virgin nature and the expanse of ocean had aroused in my mind? Never had I felt more hopelessly astray in the world of busy human activities than on this particular morning. My most heartfelt wish was to leave it all behind me; to seek once again the green shadows of the wilderness. There, perhaps, my physical welfare might be endangered; but for my soul there would open the pathway that leads to peace.

Soon, however, I began to feel that this longing was merely the expression of an impulse towards flight. I

AN INDIAN JOURNEY

began to feel that there were duties awaiting me in another land; in a realm with whose forces and aims I was associated by birth and training. For the first time after several years, my eyes turned homewards across the sea. I recalled that the man with whom for some time I had been peculiarly intimate, was full of a painful conviction that his own race was decadent; I remembered that he had spoken with enthusiasm of the future that awaited my own people; and I felt the vigour of his faith glowing in my mind with the promise of a mighty heritage.

The incidents of the day accorded with Mangeshe Rao's expectations. At noon a subaltern accompanied by three privates called at the house. He discharged his duty with as much self-importance as if he had been the king of England. When, therefore, he ceremoniously asked for my pocketknife, I handed it him with a flourish, as if I had been surrendering a sword. He could not help laughing, and seemed to become aware that a civilian was not one of his men, and that a German was not a British subject. Moreover, I had reminded him that suspicion is not proof, and that I was not myself a suspect document.

He fully resumed his official manner when the papers were discovered, and at his request I accompanied him to headquarters in a bullock cart. On the way he was perfectly civil, calm and grave in his manner. I, meanwhile, was secretly congratulating myself upon the success of my friend's strategem. After this invasion of the private rights of a number of the inhabitants of Mangalore, the military mission had suddenly assumed a far more important aspect. From the windows of Government House I could see the low, angular outlines of a gunboat, black and threatening on the quiet, blue sea, as if sketched with charcoal. The courtyard of the building was swarming with soldiers. For a moment I was seriously concerned about Mangeshe Rao's fate. When we are not behind the scenes, immediate impressions are peculiarly forcible. I was haunted by the memory of Panya's pale visage when I had left him standing as if petrified at the garden gate. I did not know whether he had understood my parting words that he was to expect me home in the evening, and I was seriously afraid lest he should commit some piece of heroic stupidity.

I was kept waiting two hours, and whiled away the time conversing with the sentinel, first fortifying his belief in witches and evil spirits by telling him blood-curdling tales of the jungle, and then calming the man's fears with cigarettes. At length, the Collector appeared, accompanied by the English colonel, to whom the civilian official was surety for my innocence. Obviously my case had been fully discussed. The Collector was apologetic, though a trifle annoyed. He remembered that it was through his instrumentality that I had made Mangeshe Rao's acquaintance, and he did not think there had been time for me to develop into a dangerous conspirator. The impression produced on my mind was that Mangeshe Rao was to be shielded. A private was sent to fetch my horse, and I was dismissed with scant ceremony. It seemed that people had more important things to think of.

Panya welcomed my return with delight, a little

AN INDIAN JOURNEY

ashamed of his fears now that I had come back safe and sound. But neither his joy nor my own relief put an end to my anxiety.

In the evening I despatched the boy to Mangeshe Rao's. The Brahmin was not at home. I gathered that he had not been arrested, but I could not make up my mind whether this was a reason for satisfaction or fresh concern.

In my memory of these anxious hours one irrelevant incident remains as vivid as if it had been the centre of the whole trouble. During the brief twilight, when the moon was already shining, I was smoking a cigar on the veranda when I perceived a shadow moving near the garden gate. At first I thought this of no importance, but at length I called Panya. Going to the gate, the boy brought back with him a child who stood looking at me in silence. She was a girl of about thirteen, clad in a red smock. Her hair was loose, and from her general aspect she must have belonged to one of the lower castes. With Panya's aid I learned the history and the wishes of this late visitor. With a hidden shudder I looked upon her with very different eyes when I knew that a few days previously she had become a mother. Those only who are familiar with the frequency of such occurrences in tropical India could have credited the fact without astonishment. This child-mother had come from a riverside village to ask my aid. She had mistaken my house for the missionary settlement.

"This is the night of free love in her village," explained Panya. "In her caste, for one night in spring, both wives and maids must give themselves to any man who wants to possess them. The village is in a turmoil all the night through, with a clamour like that of people struggling in a bog, sentenced to everlasting lust. This continues till sunrise. Then all is still, and the people sleep throughout the day. This child has run away in terror."

Panya took the young mother to the mission school, and I was left alone with the cicadas in the brilliant moonlit night—the last night in India I can distinctly remember, for when day next broke I stood beside the dead body of Mangeshe Rao.

I recall mounting my horse in the grey of morning, buttoning my coat as I rode, and becoming aware that I had forgotten my sun-helmet. I remember thinking that on my way back I should need to be careful to keep in the shade; and I remember the strange tones of Panya's voice as he spoke to my horse, running his hand on the bridle. He called out loudly when a bullock cart blocked our way near the city gate, and I saw a little hunchback, the driver, with a timid and subservient though ruffled mien, who guided his beasts into the ditch. The cart was laden with ears of maize. When the oxen were slow to move, the driver angrily kicked them in the flanks with his naked feet. Surely Panya had just cried to me in that same strange voice: "The Brahmins have poisoned Mangeshe Rao!"

It was not yet quite light when we reached the dead man's house. The well-beaten clay in front of the veranda was damp with dew; some white goats were tethered to the fence; the foliage of the palm trees rustled in the morning breeze. I heard a monotonous lamentation; sighs

AN INDIAN JOURNEY

following one another breath by breath. My first thought was: He is not dead after all; I shall still see him alive.

Round the door of the death chamber dark figures were hovering. I looked into the room to see, close by the window, a low couch on which the morning glimmer was falling, greenish and pale, like that of an almost exhausted electric torch. Beneath white draperies I could discern the twisted outlines of a human form. One hand, or rather a clenched fist, had escaped from the coverings. Waxen in tint, it was thrusting upwards in the livid light of dawn.

I drew back the shroud, but instantly replaced it over the distorted countenance. The deadly poison to which the Brahmin had succumbed was unmistakable in its effects, and manifested the malice of those who had brewed the potion in the name of their deities, degraded now to the level of spiteful idols. As I turned away, I met Panya's eyes, and when he caught sight of my face he threw himself on the ground as if felled by a blow, and broke into an animal-like howl.

In the bazaar, the motley life of the new day had begun. Nude brown figures were moving busily to and fro in the customary fashion; some were bending under burdens, while others had an upright and dignified carriage. A Mohammedan trader from whom I had promised to buy some ginger to take home with me, followed me a long way. Beside the temple, where a white wall was reflected in a pool, a pilgrim was preaching. The streets had just been watered, and the vapour that rose from them was charged with the reek of oxen. The sun was aglare; the palm trees

AN INDIAN JOURNEY

towered tranquilly above the bustle of the streets and the flat white roofs of the houses. It was growing hot.

When we reached the avenue of tall palm trees leading down to the sea, and when the murmur of the city had been replaced by the plash of the waves, I dismounted, sent Panya home with the horse, and strode forwards alone. Lassitude, laving body and soul as with a stream of bitter waters, overpowered me for a space. I closed my eyes, leaning against a tree trunk.

In a vision I saw a village of my German homeland, in the calm eventide. An elder tree was blossoming in the hedge; there had been a shower, and the air was moist and cool. Perched on the gable of a farm house, a blackbird was singing in the rays of the setting sun, and the clear sweetness of the tones filled with happiness the quiet countryside.

THE END

www.ingramcontent.com/pod-product-compliance
Lightning Source LLC
Chambersburg PA
CBHW032019230426
43671CB00005B/136